25 Lessons Learned
from 50 years in Hi Tech

a personal and professional journey
1962-2012

R. K. Wilson

Copyright © 2012 R.K Wilson

All rights reserved.

ISBN: **149538733X**
ISBN-13: **978-1495387333**

DEDICATION

This book is dedicated to my family. During this journey they experienced 16 long distance moves, changes in schools and Dad's many nights away on business travel or months away at the place of the "new move". Thanks, Barb, Derek and Carrie for your patience and forgiveness.

Babbage Difference Engine   1833

CONTENTS

1	Introduction	3-8
2	Background a company by company review	9-50
3	Lessons 1 & 2 Preparation	51-55
4	Lessons 3 & 4 Personal lessons	57-65
5	Lessons 5,6 &7 Sales & Sales Mgmt	66-74
6	Lessons 8-13 Product Mgmt, GM/Pres/CEO	75-90
7	Lessons 14-17 Strategic Planning	92-106
8	Lessons 18-20 Decision Making	107-115
9	Lessons 21-22 Agreements, MOUs & NDAs	116-121
10	Lesson 23 Negotiating a Sale or Merger	122-127
11	Lesson 24 Startups & Funding Sources	128-134
12	Lesson 25 Employee Motivation	135-140

13	Extra Lesson Doing Business in China	141-145
14	Perspective & Exhibits	146-165

University Computer Room Workstations

ACKNOWLEDGMENTS

Many thanks to those who spent the time to edit and offer suggestions –
Jim Ashbrook, Derek Wilson, Carrie Friedman, Barbara Wilson

Workstation

1 INTRODUCTION
THE 50 YEAR JOURNEY

This book is the story of a personal journey and a business journey that lasted 50 years. It's a reflection on experiences and lessons learned in that journey. It may serve to add some "food for thought" for others who are now in the process of writing their story. Some details have been omitted in order to get at the point of a lesson without getting too personal about friends and associates along the way.

These lessons are not specific to the hi-tech industry though. This book is not intended to require one to be familiar with the range of technologies mentioned here, but to be exposed to just enough of the technology background to help bring out the meat of the lessons. Certainly, as I looked back on this writing, I believe that if you have never worked in the computer technology business the lesson would remain true for most product and service businesses.

This story begins when a boy from a small town in

Kansas had a desire to "see the world" after college, and find out what he really wanted to do for his life's work. His parents, although providing a good home, love and moral support could not help with college expenses or provide counsel on his life journey. He would have to go it alone. Most of the expenses of college covered from various jobs (including working as an oil well roust-about in the oil fields of Oklahoma in the summer – where he discovered what he didn't want to do for a living), and several scholarships.

Earning a degree in Industrial Management – a combination of engineering and business, seemed to support his notion of being willing to go either way in his work life. No decisions made at this point. Interviews during college senior year included Armstrong Cork and IBM. Both seemed interesting and the prospect of finally getting a paycheck after 4 ½ years of college was a strong motivator.

IBM offered a unique opportunity to see the insides of different businesses as an IBM Systems Engineer in the Data Products Division. Also, IBM had the reputation as a company that continually educated their employees – not only about their products and technologies but about the details of an industry. For example, there were in-depth classes on banking, public utilities, medical, manufacturing, etc. So, the IBM offer was accepted without much awareness of what was about to start – a 50+ year journey through a wide swath of the computer industry.

This journey would include positions from systems engineering, sales, to management at the product marketing level to general management, VP, and company president. My intent, after about half of this journey, was to be well grounded in the skills I would need to be effective in founding and running a company. It was after almost 10 years in IBM, that I learned that I needed to set personal goals to see if I was on track with where I desired to be. So, I came up with three questions I asked myself usually once each year, and I have continued asking myself those questions along my entire journey;

1. Are you learning anything?

2. Are you having any fun?

3. Are you making any money?

The order was important to me.

The journey included working in major companies like IBM, DataQuest, Intel, National Advanced Systems (National Semi), Motorola and Computer Associates and a number of smaller companies. There were positions with P&L responsibility in two of the major companies in addition to several of the startups. The desire to build and grow a new company resulted in working in, or founding, six startups.

Also along the journey, I had the opportunity to participate in selling two companies, purchasing one and doing the "Wall Street tour" to get funding for a spin-out of a division.

Lots of lessons learned, sometimes more than once. Learning the same lesson more than once -that's the hard way – it has consequences. But as you will learn, this journey was not always in an up and ascending vector – meaning there were ups, downs and sideways moves along the way in this career. However, these bumps may have made the lessons stick. The reason for writing these lessons down is to relive what was learned. Hopefully, this will be a way of finding the value of all of that effort, long hours, travel, crisis handling and the many family disruptions along the way.

Each of the lessons outlined in this book was learned from personal experience, and by "rubbing minds" with some of the industry's best and brightest. Some were peers, some were my managers and some worked for me – but all gave insight and new ideas and approaches and criticisms. The lessons that were actually used in the performance of my work, and proved to be effective, are in this book. Some of the lessons are meant to illustrate, where if not cautious, you may be the odd man out when trotting out your "world beating idea". The reader may find that some lessons seem obvious and too simple, but, dedicated to the execution of an obvious and simple idea may be the key to its success.

As you read on, you may feel like you are getting a bit of a computer industry history lesson. But in a journey of 50 plus years, the history may provide some context for the lessons chapters. When I began my journey, IBM was selling unit record accounting machines and some mainframes and other computers that were incompatible with each other. That meant the programs on one would not run on others – islands of computing and systems design. Accounting machines were massive (heavy) machines that used 80 column cards for input. Now we have more memory, storage and computing power in our hand-held devices, and we can communicate world-wide and utilize the cloud.

The world of computing devices now touches everyone from the 4 year old, to the 90 year old. We have witnessed the most rapid development of technology in human history. That was the backdrop for this personal and business journey.

So technology has marched on to where we find ourselves today – almost all social connections are from machine to machine or device to device. Once it could be said that hell is a place where everything connects to nothing, <u>but now</u> it may be described as where everything connects to everything.

I hope you find my business journey interesting, and the lessons learned helpful.

2 BACKGROUND
A COMPANY BY COMPANY OVERVIEW

During my journey there were many companies, dozens of products and technologies and 16 long distance moves.

Why so many companies? Was I a job hopper always looking for higher income? First, let me take you on a quick overview of some of the companies and products in my journey. Then I think the obvious answer is that I was being true to my three personal goals.

I worked for IBM for over 13 years, from the early '60's until the mid '70's. At IBM I was a systems engineer, salesman, education manager and marketing manager in the Data Processing Division.

Notable events while at IBM
The introduction of the Gene Amdahl inspired systems 360 family of computers. The 360 was the first family of

computers that were compatible across a broad range of computing power. Before that each IBM system's programs would not execute on different computer models. So this was a giant step in the industry, and began a growth spurt for IBM.

The '60s was the era of the introduction of virtual storage and memory paging. The concept of virtual storage facilitated the running of multiple processes or programs at the same time by swapping out program segments to storage and swapping in needed new ones as needed. Computers with this capability simply made expensive real hardware memory appear to be virtually unlimited in size – "Virtual". It also helped in taking the lid off the size of programs.

Met T.J. Watson Jr one day in our IBM office in Kansas City: He traveled around to various offices unannounced, to have one-on-one conversations with IBMers. I had the opportunity for one of those face-to-face meetings. I found him to be delightful, but I was petrified I would say something that might ditch my career. By the way, in the earliest days of mainframe computers, Watson is attributed to the quote, "The world will not need more than five of these massive machines." I don't think this is an accurate quote from Watson, but is does illustrate that the forecasting was way off. Not too many good tools for forecasting in those early days I suppose.

I had heard about unfortunate employees getting a "Watson letter", which was written to salesmen whose customers had communicated to IBM about something they were not happy with, and the letter, of course, referenced their salesman. Watson would then write the infamous "Watson letter" to the subject salesman. No one wanted to get a Watson letter.

I taught *IBM Sales and Marketing School*, as well as *Marketing in the '70s*. The *Marketing in the '70s* curriculum provided information on how a business could financially justify and compute the return on its computer purchases. IBM felt that buying computers (and other hardware and software) was becoming increasingly the job of financial managers. These corporate managers were increasingly being tasked with proving financial justification for the purchases or leases of newer and larger machines.

The sales and marketing classes were two or three weeks long and for each class there was an election of class officers. **In those days, women in IBM, if they were in sales, were always on teams – with other IBM men.** In one of the classes there was a woman running for a class officer. On the morning of the election of officers each candidate was allowed a short speech. When it was the turn for the lady mentioned above to give her "vote for me speech", I was totally unprepared for the speech she was about to give in this straight-laced IBM culture.

She walked up to the podium carrying a small sack, and as she stood behind the podium she began draping men's ties over the podium until there were seven ties draped over it. Then she said, "I was doing a little campaigning last night and I know I've got at least seven votes". The audience howled and she got elected – guess it was time for a new IBM culture.

As a marketing manager, I hired and managed; the first new business saleswoman in IBM (at least I was told this at the time); and for one year, managed the second highest performing new business salesman in IBM.

The best one liner I think I ever heard was delivered by a black IBM Systems Engineer. It was in the early '70s and he was the only black engineer in the Knoxville, TN office at the time. One day the salesman and I were to introduce him as the new S.E. on an account that was in the planning stages of accepting a new IBM system. The customer was a genuine "redneck" sort of CEO often found in the south at that time. As we three walked in, dressed in our IBM attire – dark suits, white shirts, stripped ties and wing tip shoes, the face of the CEO reddened and his jaw dropped. This might be a tense meeting. As we were sitting down and without a minute's hesitation the new S.E. said. "I know what you're thinking....all us IBMers look alike." That was the best ice breaker I think I have ever heard. From that day forward his color was no issue in that business and with that CEO.

The best new business salesman, I ever observed was a new business salesman under my charge in Knoxville. Not only was he the number two best in the IBM company, he did it with a boon dock territory that was in Tennessee and Kentucky. When going on sales calls with Steve M., we did a lot of driving to places that were remote, non-union, and therefore unnamed manufacturing plants. Whenever Steve met a new prospect he introduced himself as "I am Steve M., from Strawberry Plains, Tennessee, and I am your IBM rep". He had to get that good 'ole boy reference in there and it worked for him in Tennessee.

Now, I must tell you that on all of my calls with Steve it was obvious that he had what we used to call "account control". His customers saw Steve as one of them, and someone who was looking out for their welfare in the use of the IBM computers he sold them. One day just before the 4th of July, we went to call on the DP manager of a wholesale liquor distributor. They were having trouble converting from a previous system to the newly delivered new IBM system. This was their busiest time of the year and the new system was having installation problems. Steve had orchestrated the service engineers and the systems engineers in a gallant effort to make the new system work and to allow the customer to get the products shipped and billed in this busy season. Well, by shear brute force effort, the IBM people he had on site together with the customer people on hand, went back to the more manual, old system, to get the bills out. Then the DP manager came up, obviously disappointed in having to go back to the old system and said to Steve; "I'm sorry Steve, I feel like I have let you down". What? What did she just say?

She was essentially addressing Steve as if he were the president of the company instead of their IBM salesman. That described how much HE was perceived as having as much to do with the success of the company as any employee. Of course, the work got out, the day was saved, and the new system was soon up and running perfectly a day later. But the crisis was met and handled.

I got a Watson letter. In Tennessee there were many garment manufacturers, and several of these were IBM customers. One of these clients was a successful shirt manufacturer of men's and women's shirts. The company was run by a lady (should I say an Iron Lady). It was the '70s and shirts for both men and women were mostly colored shirts in that time – not white. Of course my salesman and I would call on this company with our required IBM attire which dictated a white shirt. One day the lady owner called us into her office where she had a display of many of their current products and said, "look at the shirts we are making and selling today. Do you see any white ones? I think IBM should get with the current fashion and I am going to tell your president so." We agreed she was much more in fashion than we were and we vowed to her NEVER to come into her business again with a white shirt on. We changed in the car before entering the plant after that.

Well, she did write that letter anyway, and we got the feared Watson letter in return. It was not so serious however, because the Watson letter to us commended us for being sensitive to our customer's request. Whew!

The IBM dress code was a curiosity to some of people of east Tennessee. A brand new salesman asked me to go on calls with him in some of the smaller towns in his rural territory. We planned to leave early one morning and head to Jamestown, Tennessee. For those that may not be aware, Tennessee has two time zones. Our office in Knoxville was in the Eastern time zone and farther west in Tennessee was the Midwest time zone. Actually, we were not aware that the time in Jamestown was an hour behind our time.

So, we arrived an hour too early and decided to have coffee in a small cafe in Jamestown town square.

While drinking our coffee and discussing the day ahead, it became apparent that everyone in the cafe was looking at us. Finally, one gentleman who had obviously noticed we were the only ones in town with dark suits and white shirts, came over to talk. He said, "Say are you fellas new in town? By the way you are dressed you must be either here for preachin' or undertakin' ". Wow! Those IBM togs can really get you noticed in rural Tennessee.

Introduction of the IBM 370 family: This new compatible family of increased power and capability was announced in 1970. The most notable part of this announcement to me was the protracted delivery schedule for the many customers who ordered S/370 machines. I was not alone in having customers with delivery dates 30 – 36 months out. Try working that one with your customers!

The radioactive computer system: I had to put this one in because I had never heard this happening either before or since. Most people have probably heard of Oak Ridge, Tennessee outside of Knoxville. It was a secret atomic energy research facility of all underground labs with cryptic names like K25 and F17 (the names don't matter but I am sure K25 was one of the lab facilities). In one of those underground labs was a <u>leased</u> IBM 1800 system. We got a call from Union Carbide (the contracted source for work at the lab) one day that the 1800 system had become radioactively contaminated. The result was that they needed to buy it, bury it and buy its replacement. Wonder what happened with the operators? A good day for an IBM salesman!

After three positions in the Systems Division that moved me to Washington DC, Knoxville, TN and back to Kansas City; I realized that my view of how a company's business really worked, was still much too limited. Furthermore, how do you really make your mark in a company that size with so many competent people entrenched in jobs above you? There must be a more wide-ranging view of a tech company's business out there for me. A small company with potential might be the right direction to go. Besides, I would be able to get in on its growth and have potential to get a larger perspective of the business.

After a long 13 plus year career at IBM I found I was not meeting all of my personal Objectives, so I began to look at other opportunities. A recruiter pointed me to **Decision Data** which was about to announce some low-end systems, and that was a sharp contrast with IBM mainframes, peripherals and software. Also, it didn't seem like I would be competing directly with "mother

IBM". Believe it or not, this was a key factor in my decision.

But, after two and a half years, there was still no systems announcement from the company, and again a recruiter interested me in a position with an IBM plug compatible computer company in San Diego – **National Advanced Systems , NAS,** (a subsidiary company of National Semi). It was the late 1970's, and this was to be my first experience inside a plant with design engineering, manufacturing and product and strategic marketing – a totally new view and perspective. Great!

To back up a minute, what is an IBM plug compatible machine (PCM)? Basically, the systems we were building would run all of the software that the IBM mainframes would run, but were designed with newer technology resulting in smaller and less expensive systems of equal or greater performance.

Itel was our OEM for the mainframes we designed and built. Itel used to tout that they would be the first hi-tech company to reach $1 billion in revenue in less than ten years. At one point, Itel was shipping almost as many of the PCM (plug compatible mainframes) per month as IBM was shipping IBM labeled mainframes.

They were living a grand and lavish life style – luxurious offices, high compensation plans and Ferrari and

Mercedes as company cars for sales and management. Itel even owned a villa in South America – not sure why but I would bet it was for customer entertainment of the highest order.

Some lessons regarding marketing, positioning and competitive analysis would be learned here.

The IBM compatible and add-on memory business was a great business and very profitable – and then it happened. IBM was taking too many losses and was getting smarter. I remember while at IBM, that they would react to competition only when that competition was responsible for too many lost sales.

You might wonder how a company could build a better IBM mainframe out of different parts and still remain software compatible. The answer in those days was the IBM logic manuals kept in every customer mainframe site. IBM field service engineers used these logic manuals to trouble shoot and repair or replace parts. The system's design was right there in those manuals! All one had to do is have a mainframe site or two and you had the manuals at your site.

I do remember that IBM began getting smarter when the intelligent console code for the largest systems was not on site – i.e, not in the logic manuals. That created a tough one for our engineers. If you remember your history, you may remember that Hitachi Japan (and also Amdahl/Fujitsu) were also building IBM compatible disk and tape peripherals and large mainframes. Hitachi was sued by IBM for industrial espionage regarding mainframe intellectual property in the late '70's and the case was not settled until 1983.

Then the IBM 4300 announcements were made in 1979 with follow-on announcements of additional models. All were competitors to systems we were building and what Itel was selling, with lower price and better environmental features. These new systems did not need the expensive data center environment and cooling. It changed the mainframe price equation. The amount of an installed systems residual value went down significantly.

Itel sold customer lease paper to companies that factored the lease paper and gave Itel the cash up front – but counting on a certain residual value at the end of the lease. So, a customer's leased system from Itel, could no longer command the "guaranteed" residual value. Itel was on the hook with their leasing company partners. Itel also had systems in inventory and on order from NAS, and the IBM announcement stopped all customer orders while customers tried to figure out what to lease or buy. This customer hiatus killed Itel cash flow and dropped the residual value of installed Itel systems in their installed base. Itel had agreements with customers assuring those residual amounts.

This "disaster in the wings" was not a surprise, but the lack of readiness by Itel was a surprise. This was the blow that killed Itel and put NAS into the direct sales and service of systems. In less than a year, NAS using Itel's sales and service force, transitioned completely to a Hitachi systems line and their peripherals. No need any longer for design and manufacturing of systems by NAS in San Diego, and layoffs resulted.

It was the Spring of 1980 and I was out of a job, when another recruiter rode to the rescue. Intel (not to be confused with Itel), was building a systems division that was based in Phoenix. The division's products were very different than traditional Intel products. The Systems Division products included mainframe add-on memory products, IBM channel attached solid state storage (i.e. memory based), Xenix systems, mainframe Data Base products, and other mainframe software.

I consider my time at Intel some of my most productive and rewarding of my career. The Intel Systems Division was involved in designing, manufacturing, selling and servicing Unix-based systems hardware and software and a host of mainframe related products including Database software, add-on memory, and a fast peripheral storage device that was made of Intel memory chips and would emulate an IBM disk or drum device. Intel also had some interesting LAN networking products and a leading edge speech recognition and synthesis product. Not at all what I expected to find Intel involved in. In my time at Intel I was in Marketing or General Management for all of these systems products.

Eventually, I also became responsible for the Speech Inspection unit. This was an interesting time. Intel was not on the approved vendor list at GM and had great desire to sell product into GM. The team had developed a very leading edge application for the speech product – inspection stations. Auto inspectors were prompted via speech synthesis on "what to inspect" and speech recognition in the system to understand the operator's inspection comments. All of this with wireless communication in an auto plant. Not a friendly place for wireless communication – but it worked. Intel management felt this product installed in some GM auto plans could serve to get Intel on the preferred vendor list.

Several GM plants and other companies like Kodak used the system to wirelessly communicate the important quality inspection information and to make decisions on correcting manufacturing errors in time to save lots of money and rework. And of course, this demonstrated why GM must put Intel on that coveted list - and so they were.

Based on our experience with products attached to IBM mainframe channels, sprang an idea for a new product. Together with a small team of Intel engineers and marketing folks, a business plan for that idea was developed over Christmas holidays one year. That product began as an internal start-up inside Intel, and became known as **FastPath**. The idea was interesting because at the time, any device other than an IBM device (disk, tape etc. or plug compatible peripheral) could only communicate with the mainframe at the speed of a terminal – not at channel speed. Even some IBM devices like the series 1 system needed a "Fastpath" into the mainframe. With IBM, GE and others ordering prototypes, the new operation became fully funded by Intel. I think this was only the third internal startup Intel had done to that point. One of the fabulously successful internal start-ups was the PC enhancement operation – the number two Intel internal start-up.

I met and worked with Gordon Moore (of Moore's Law fame and a founder of Intel), Andy Grove, Andy Bryant, Mat Diethelm, John McNulty and many other talented folks at Intel.

Intel had a company culture led by Grove that seemed to promote productivity and innovation. (More about this in the lessons chapters)

Notable events while at Intel

The large semiconductor competition: In the early '80's Intel felt threatened by the larger Japanese companies and by US based Texas Instruments. This caused a number of initiatives to promote longer work hours (the 125% solution to work 25% more hours per week at the same pay) and to reduce costs (the 90% solution - a reduction in pay of 10%). It worked, and new products got out on time and expenses were reduced to help the bottom line.

Solid state disk resurrection: After less than a year at Intel, I was asked to take over the solid state disk product line that attached to mainframe channels. Only one problem! The product was introduced, installed and had failed and was removed in a major customer name in the oil industry. So realistically we had no product – just some serious design issues. But, after some reworking the design with some excellent Intel engineers we had a new product with a new look that was bullet proof. It actually was.

Solid state disk is created with non-volatile memory chips as its storage, and we had extra memory on board that would automatically configure itself to replace any failing memory locations – so we billed it as self-healing or bullet proof. This product was designed to attach to an IBM mainframe (or PCM) channel and emulate an IBM drum so it would function as a faster "drum" and at channel speeds. This was a breakthrough for virtual system paging (moving program segments in/out of main system memory), and because of its enhanced performance, datacenters could get better response time to on-line users and more online users than with IBM products. Even IBM data centers liked the product and were buying it.

Intel first lease program: The SSD products were not typical Intel prices – they ranged from $125,000 to $500,000 in purchase price. Datacenter users were accustomed to IBM's buy or lease for their products, so the first Intel leasing program was established for this operation. I was already familiar with the leasing companies we might do business with from my NAS experience. The solid state disk operation became extremely profitable with its combination of lease and purchase product portfolio, and one year became a major contributor to Intel's pre-tax profit.

Database sale: One turn-around leads to another. Intel had a mainframe system database company they had previously purchased in Austin, Texas. It had developed products for IBM, CDC and Sperry systems called System

2000 or S2K, that were well accepted in the market- i.e. the cash cow product. However, Intel wanted to use their expertise to build a database backend processor out of Intel chips to offload DB processing from the host and to theoretically increase the much sought after highest "transactions per second". After attempting to create the database transaction computer, it failed to provide the performance goals and was abandoned. Intel suggested I move to Austin and turn it around. Really? **Here is a good lesson** – when you abandon your cash cow product to put your entire energy into a "dream product" you may get caught with your cash cow down (or almost dead).

That was exactly the situation. Competition had moved on to the new industry buzz word in databases – relational. Intel-Austin's S2K product had no answer with its hierarchical database products. With some good consultant help the current products were analyzed to determine how much and how long it would take to be competitive. Then the decision would be develop or sell before it was too late.

The sell option became obvious choice if the right buyer could be found. There was a large installed base of S2K customers that was attractive to potential buyers but also a potential negative for Intel if not served well by a new owner.

Customers expect product support even if/when a new company takes over the product line.

It took about nine months to find a buyer that met our criteria; which were:

1. Take care of the installed customers, and avoid legal action.
2. Buyer must keep enough employees that would allow sufficient customer support.

3. Take a cadre of the existing employees to Phoenix to support the Xenix systems software requirements there.

4. Provide some cash to Intel.

Unix-based file servers operation profitable: After the sale of the Austin database operation, it was back to Phoenix with 26 engineers to work on the file server products and the solid state memory devices. This operation had never really gotten off the ground sufficiently to make it profitable. But with some tremendous effort of sales opening up government customers and manufacturing grinding down costs, the operation made a profit within a year.

Internal start-up: About this time, Intel realized that engineers, marketers and managers were being attracted to the swelling number of Silicon Valley startups. So Intel launched a program for startup ideas to be funded internally. These internal startups would be treated just like VC funded companies on the outside – VC funding depending on hitting milestones and startup employees to receive a share of the ventures success. In the fall of '85 there were two such internal startups already underway.

Seeing the two other Intel internal startups being launched, just whetted my appetite for doing a startup. With the ability to draft off of the engineering expertise of the solid state disk work, the idea of the FastPath product was born. It became funded for prototyping and generating interest. Then after key customers placed orders, it became fully funded for production. All of this happened in less than six months.

First international business travel: Because the products I was responsible for were sold internationally, I was able to travel for business to Japan and Western Europe. Intel had sales and service for our systems products in those regions of the world and on many occasions I had the opportunity to work with our international sales/service people and our customers and prospects. It was great that finally some international flavor added. The "see the world itch" was finally being scratched.

At the end of life for our solid state disk products I had

the opportunity to negotiate and sell the European installed base of product and accompanying spares to Memorex Europe. (a negotiation lesson learned in the process).

Worked with three Intel CEOs
During my time at Intel, I had the opportunity to work with Gordon Moore, Andy Grove and Craig Barrett. Each of them served as President and CEO either while I was at Intel or just shortly after I left.

Those darn head hunters
Although, I was not looking, along came another recruiter. He wove an enticing story about how I could potentially run a company that he knew of (ECD). The president/ founder had a tremendous number of products (mostly prototypes or lab demonstrations) based on amorphous material technology. A really new area for me to explore, and since the president was getting older, who would help make his work and the work of the company's 100 or so PHDs a reality? It took some persuading for me to leave Intel and move to Detroit – as it should. Never the less, after visiting Detroit one beautiful spring weekend (very few days like that) with my wife, I agreed to make the move.

It was here I got exposed to color LCD displays employing leading edge (at the time) active matrix technology. This technology had been developed by a division of ECD (the company) and had been funded by them. So why not spin out this division and get the funds required to commercialize the LCD product? It was then that I began to learn why the president really wanted me there. He had essentially been "black listed" by Wall Street for over hyping his company and its technology, so would not be welcomed to do the Wall Street tour to raise money. The chief scientist and I began the NY, Boston, Philadelphia and Minneapolis tour presenting the technology to the investment houses.

Notable events while at ECD
Spin off of LCD division: Well, it must have worked because we raised over $23M to spin out the LCD division as a separate company – it really was a startup after a period of in-house funding. A lesson or two learned from this experience.

Back to Silicon Valley – president of a start-up
Another recruiter persuaded me to serve as president of a true, seeking VC capital start-up. Because I did not see any future for me to become the President of the company - that I now knew too much about, I was anxious to get back to the Silicon Valley scene where in the late "80s startup activity was blooming and booming.

Little did I know, that my next stint would last only a few months. A very interesting startup based on a system of multiple Intel processors offered me the position as president – had ego appeal. It was late September of 1987 and the company had not produced a business plan to shop to venture capital companies in the valley. Angel funding had sustained the company thus far, but real capital was needed urgently - NOW. I had just left a situation where the company president could not present to the Wall Street financiers, and now I find a similar one. In this case the company was founded by an individual who had a reputation for loosing hundreds of millions of venture dollars in a previous venture that had failed. So again, get a fresh face to attack the ramparts of venture capital.

Positioning the technology and its importance in the market was the task of the business plan. After a cursory "drive by" of the venture folks we began working on some of the changes they suggested – primarily positioning the product in the market.

Then, the October 19th 1987 market crash (named Black Monday) happened and there were no VCs to be found for about a year. I could not hold my breath that long and of course didn't know how long the hiatus would last. Here is where your friends can help you. A friend I had worked with in San Diego told me I should apply to DataQuest, because they were looking for a VP/GM to run their Systems Division.

DataQuest

For those that may not know the name DataQuest, they and Gartner Group were the key information services providers to the computing industry in the late '80s and early '90s, and also did a lot of "one off" consulting for the industry's computer, communication and software companies. I remember an interesting visit from many of the financial institutions of India seeking counsel on what part the country could play in the computer and/or software industry. Should they focus resources on a hardware niche or what? At the end of the day after a presentation covering a "state of the union" on almost all of the segments we covered, it was suggested that they might find most success in software.

There were several reasons for that.
1. They had no base of manufacturing that would have supported hardware device production

2. Software development generally has a shorter time to develop and get to market

3. They speak English and would develop software and documentation in English for a market that mostly spoke English.

4. The country had an abundance of well-educated engineers.

In hind sight that seems to have been good direction – India has developed world –leading software outsourcing companies.

This was a fun job. Because of the conferences and constant stream of companies, VCs, and start-ups coming thru to speak with us and get opinions; it was extremely informative about who is doing what in the industry. Of course, all that did was whet my appetite for the start-up fever again.

Notable events while at DataQuest: It was the late "80s and early '90s and the Systems Division included research work on the emerging local area network (LAN) companies. This was a "big bang" event in the industry. It fostered Cisco and many new companies and allowed for the effectiveness of distributed computing. All of this helped promote the business we were doing in research on related technologies with vendors and customers.

Each year DataQuest held international conferences in Japan, Europe and Korea. So this allowed me the opportunity to present in those conferences as well as personally visit companies following the conference that wanted to ask their sensitive business questions.

Japan led the way on this one – not only the computing related companies were requesting visits but also those large industrial companies that felt they should have a place in the computing industry. Sort of a "here's our idea – what do you think" session.

In my Japan travels to client companies, I was always accompanied by one of our employees from the Tokyo office. On one occasion, I was being "tended" by a very personable Tokyo employee. He did a very good job of getting me on and off the right trains and to the right business locations except for one time. At the end of a long day of interviews and travel, we were on our way on, I thought, our last train leg of the trip. The train pulled into a station and my guide said to stay on – funny, everyone else got off. After several minutes he realized his error and said " go off now"! He explained later that the train's next stop was train car storage, a remote location where we did not want to be.

An information start-up
An information services startup idea: After about two years of successful operation of the Systems Group at DataQuest, I saw an opportunity for producing more, and more effective, information about end customers for the vendor companies than DQ or any services provider was doing at the time. The idea was to use on-line data gathering from some of the best-of-breed end user companies to interview <u>and</u> compile what made them more successful users of leading technologies of the day.

What could be learned from the top 20% that would help the other 80%? Customers educating customers seemed like information valuable to vendors and customers alike. Although DQ blessed my idea and provided non-financial help in getting to VC's; the VC's did not see the great dollar multiple return they desire – so no funding here. But I had worked on, and designed the programs for almost a year. It is interesting to note that I called my new venture TAP for Technology Access Program, and several years later I met with the president of TIP. This company was founded to do almost exactly the same thing and had a very similar name. When I saw their presentations, I felt I was reliving mine. Their funding came from Gartner Group I believe – which later bought DQ.

When all else fails – consult: What do you sometimes do when the startup doesn't start? Many times you use the experience and contacts you have to consult. Together with a friend who was already involved in doing some consulting, we took it on. During this time, my friend was already taking advantage of having access to a U.S.-wide database of all installed hardware and software as well as contact information for the IT management at each location.

This proved to be a great tool for providing vendors custom interviews with end user IT management about the hardware and software they were using - what they liked and disliked and what their next moves might be. This was conducted via intelligent interviews not surveys. Interviews with the right IT people, guided by people (us) that understood the technology and would know if the IT professional had not understood the question correctly, and based on answers we got, we could ask intelligent follow-on questions.

Notable events while performing independent consulting
It is interesting that for more than a year of consulting of the type described, there develops a unique way of interfacing to the vendor execs that are sponsoring the consulting interviews. They get to know you and appreciate your expertise. One vendor hired us for a year-long separate contract prior to the launch of a new product.

On another consulting assignment, I was consulted on the best tactics to pull application programs and file systems off the mainframes for their move to distributed computing platforms. This is a lot harder than it may seem at first glance. Consider that the mainframe application programs and file systems that support those applications were developed by people who are long gone – together with their knowledge and expertise. Consider that in those file systems (not databases) there are multiple instances of the "same data" with presumably much of the same data contained in them – the process of keeping them up to date and getting to a steady state for any conversion may be almost impossible. The strategy at the time was called the "surround strategy". That meant surrounding the old applications on mainframes with new ones, or completely reworked mainframe ones on distributed servers.

Early '90s and Motorola: When operating as a consultant one is always looking for the next interesting business opportunity. A chance meeting in a restaurant in Silicon Valley led to that next opportunity. An engineer who had worked for me at Intel (ran our rapid proto skunk works in Phoenix), was still in Phoenix but now with Motorola. He was the lead on Motorola's foray into massively parallel super computers. He offered a job as the strategic marketing guy for this venture and a move back to Phoenix. I took it for a couple of reasons. I wanted to get back to an industry job (you know with benefits), and I felt the massively parallel super computer would be another opportunity to really learn something.

A system with multiple parallel processors presents some challenges. There are only a few inherently parallel applications – like processing communication packets for example. So to make such a machine more useful over a wider range of applications, the group set out to determine how to make an application parallel by allowing parallel program strings/threads to run concurrently but still keep processes in sync. Consider a program where it is important for the correct answer, that thread A complete before B which must complete before thread C in order to feed into a correct answer.

Motorola contracted with MIT to help solve that problem, and did their part by designing a feature on their 68k processor chip that allowed for message passing. This was the communication between processors that was to allow the MIT software to solve the synchronization problem.

Let me get to the end of this story quickly. Motorola ran out of money to fund this research when the operation was nearing success, and may have pulled the plug too soon. Up until then there had been keen interest from multiple national labs interested in the approach.

We were all promised other positions within Motorola. I expressed interest in a position to manage their systems group that featured a multi processor database transaction server. (Here is a lesson) If you put yourself up as a candidate and it poses a threat to one who had the inside track to the position, then you could be looked upon as an enemy. Exactly what happened. As an accommodation, I was given a strategic position to work with Group Bull of France, our partner in this product venture. The new Group Manager was never comfortable with me around and tried various tactics to make it appear I was failing in my job – unsuccessfully. This was a no win position to be in, so I began to look for another opportunity.

During my tenure at Motorola, the company seemed confused about what role if any they should have in the systems business. Should it be parallel systems, or maybe database servers or maybe just stay in mobile phones. Oh by the way, the entire systems group was run by the exec who began the mobile phone business and was chiefly responsible for its success. Not exactly the best candidate to run the systems business. I should have seen this one coming.

Notable events while at Motorola: Working with MIT and exposure to the U.S. Department of Energy Labs. Intel and IBM were also on our list of potential partners and expressed interest in the parallel system work.

While working on the parallel system, we also worked with German and French companies who were also engaged in parallel systems and software. There were interesting characters and it was an interesting time.

Group Bull (France) and Motorola developed a joint development and product agreement on the multi processor database transaction servers. On a number of occasions we visited their facilities in several parts of France and Italy to foster the cooperation.

It was the year before the 50th anniversary of D-Day, when we met with the Bull execs to kick off the joint projects. At this juncture I had the opportunity to name the overall project and the specific products. So with this background – the overall project was named Normandie (French spelling), and the products were the names of the landing beaches – Juno, Sword, Omaha …

The French had a celebration dinner for us and the featured brandy was the famous brandy from the Norman die region – Calvados. The story is that the French buried the brandy so the occupying Germans could not get it, and when the allies landed they dug it up and shared it with them. I had never heard of this brandy before, but when I returned home and was recovering from jet lag on a Sunday morning, an old Charles Boyer movie came on TV. And yes the brandy he offered the cold, and wet little French girl was – Calvados.

A fledging software start-up – CoreData
Here was a example of a software startup getting its primary funding by "bootstrapping" its financial

requirements by developing software directly for their first customer. Yes, there was a little angel (small dollar investors) funding, but mostly the cost of the program and people were from the OEM customer. They wanted to sell the software as a part of their customer offering – hence it was an OEM arrangement from us to them.

The emerging mobile workforce all with laptop computers created an opportunity for this software. How could the remote, traveling worker keep his laptop data secure and restore it if something happened that destroyed some or all of the important data on his system? That was the problem CoreData was organized to solve. From his hotel room or his next business stop, he could connect with his corporate system via the Internet or phone and with the CoreData software **only the changed bytes of data on his laptop would be backed up to his corporate server**. A restore, if necessary, could be performed in the field in a few simple steps.

Because laptop data was being lost on a regular basis – operator error or other errors damaging data, prospects all seemed to be able to identify with this issue.

I was hired to be the OEM VP sales/marketing.

Notable events while at CoreData: I think the most notable thing was that by using the revenue of OEM customers, the company was able to be **"self fueling" and profitable in less than two years.** The list of interested prospects was growing rapidly, but also the interest of some other larger companies who were potential competitors with similar solutions.

The decision was made to look for a buyer. This decision was made after investigating and rejecting the time and money it would require to take the company public (IPO). I was tasked with developing a list of potential buyers whose software products we would complement with our solution. There were some large, industry leading software companies on the list of ten potential buyers.

A successful purchase was made by Sterling Software, a company with complementary storage management software. It was a grueling process with the buyer and his 3rd party consultant. (lessons here also – how does a small company get the interest turned up in getting a buyer).

This happened in the summer of 1999 and resulted in a move to Sacramento to work for Sterling Software. I probably have never worked for a company that was as employee friendly. But this wasn't to last, because **Computer Associates (CA), purchased Sterling** in the spring of 2000.

I stayed with Sterling/Computer Associates for five years – mostly because of personal reasons. Most of my work there was in Business Development and seeking out newer companies in the areas of storage management that would be important technology adds to CA products.

Notable events while at CA:
I began the push to get CA involved in **Storage Area Networking (SANs).** There was significant interest in the market to manage these networked storage devices both for performance and risk management of storage data assets. Seems like a good extension to CA's Unicenter management product. Russ Artz was impressed with my explanation of why SANs made sense for CA and had me work directly for him for a while. Russ was one of the founders of CA.

In this function, I had a number of small companies and some large ones come into to CA in Long Island to explain their technology under non-disclosure to CA engineers. The hope was that CA would either OEM, or buy the company or its technology.

I had a lot of misgivings about the ethics of CA at that time. I felt that lapse of ethics came as a culture from the top. And during my tenure there, the president and VP of sales were convicted of fraud and paid fines and did jail time. I could see it coming.

I retired from CA with the plan in mind to begin **my last start-up venture in network security.** With a friend at CA who was Chinese, we felt we could take advantage of the low wages and manufacturing costs to engineer a security product and manufacture it in China. The intent was to sell (OEM) the product world-wide.

In order to do that, we formed a U.S. company as the sales and marketing arm, a HK company as the order processing and payment arm and a couple of companies in China to serve as in-country engineering and manufacturing. Our customers were almost exclusively outside of China – U.S., Europe, South America, Israel, Japan and Australia.

The initial funding came from the two founders. But very soon we secured orders for engineering improvements in current security products for a well-known U.S. company with a portfolio of security products. The billings from this activity (engineering and manufacturing), was sufficient to allow us to be profitable in the first full year of activity.

There were definitely some lessons learned in this venture, not the least of which concerned how to develop business as a foreign company in China.

Notable events in the China venture:
The most exciting part of this venture was to be able to

build a business to profit quickly. And then to engineer significant new products using our own developed intellectual property.

Keeping your IP yours i.e., making sure it doesn't walk out with your key employees, is the biggest challenge in China. We made some good strides here and also some mistakes.

The company still exists today, but my involvement after eight years is over.

The company name in the U.S. and Hong Kong is HierStar. It goes by several names in China for reasons I won't get into in this document, but mostly it has to do with the complications of doing business in China.

Summary: People and Places

The most delightful part of this business and life journey is the people you meet and work with, and the places your business life takes you.

Here is a short list of some of the people that made the journey meaningful.

At IBM:

Roger Mercer, my first sales branch mgr.
TJ Watson Jr, son of IBM founder
Steve M., best new business salesmen I ever worked with
Many, many others who went on to found their own companies

At NAS:
Bob Spencer, GM at NAS, and venture capital
Jim Ashbrook, product manager and later president of a software company
Floyd Kvamme, NAS and venture capital
Allan Baumgartner, strategy at NAS, and consultant

At Intel:
Gordon Moore, president, Intel chairman
Andy Grove, president of Intel
Craig Barrett, president of Intel
Andy Bryant, current board chairman of Intel
Bill Lattin, VP of Systems Group at the time
Les Vadez, charged with Intel acquisitions and internal startups

John McNulty, Intel GM, later president of several companies

At Memorex:
Clancy Spangle, president of Memorex
Al Conover, executive in charge of products

At Microsoft:
Bill Gates and Steve Balmer, both, at one time, presidents of Microsoft

At SAS:
Jim Goodnight, president of SAS

While at DataQuest:
Manny Fernandez, president of DataQuest
Vinod Kosla, SUN founder and VC
Scott McNealy, SUN founder
Larry Ellison, president of Oracle

At Motorola:
Robert Galvin, president and son of founder

At CA:
Russ Artz, a founder of CA

At west coast startup:
Carl Amdahl, president and VC (and with father Gene Amdahl started Trilogy)

At Storage Tek:
Jessie Aweida, founder of STK and other high tech companies

At ECD:
Stan Ovshinsky, president and founder
Zvi Yaniv, chief scientist on the color LCD products

Places:
My business journey afforded me the opportunity to travel and do business with executives from a number of countries including:

U.S. – major cities in most states

Western Europe – many trips to France, Denmark, Netherlands, Belgium, Monte Carlo, Germany and U.K.

Asia – Japan, Taiwan, Singapore, Hong Kong, China and Israel

The period of the late '80s to 2010 featured a number of acquisitions and mergers that shaped the industry. It was an interesting and active time for consolidations, and some of these touched me personally.

The mainframe years
The period of the "60s thru the '80s; and into the early '90s belonged to the mainframes with attached "dumb"

terminals.

The distributed computing years
In the '80s, local area networking (LANs) and servers with workstations and PCs instead of dumb terminals, became more popular including failsafe systems like Tandem and Apollo.

Networked storage years
The decade of 2000's emphasized the importance of networked storage and massive data stores and the PC's as personal work stations grew even more popular.

The internet companies years (everybody had a PC and could connect to the Internet)
The 2000's also ushered in the Internet companies and Internet applications and storage in a big way, and the previous systems and network technologies paved the way to support these on-line applications companies. It spawned acquisitions and mergers.

A few of the key acquisitions are listed below:

- 1982   - Burroughs buys Memorex
- 1986   - Burroughs acquires Sperry and names the new company Unisys
- 1989   - NAS was acquired by Hitachi & EDS and became Hitachi Data Systems

- 1989   - Apollo acquired by HP
- 1997   - Compaq buys Tandem
- 1998   - DEC purchased by Compaq
- 1998   - Netframe purchased by Micron
- 1999   - EMC buys Data General & Sequent
- 2000   - CA buys Sterling software
- 2000   - Amdahl/Fujitsu announced they were no longer putting in development dollars

- 2005   - SUN acquired Storage Tech
- 2007   - Brocade acquires McData
- 2009   - Oracle buys SUN Microsystems
- 2010   - Intel buys McAfee
- 2010   - Western Digital buys Hitachi Global Storage (not to be confused with HDS)

3 PREPARATION
LESSONS 1&2:

The previous two chapters provided me with the background and experience needed to help me realize the business lessons in this book. It is interesting, that although I worked in a number of different companies, with different technologies and different people – many of the lessons were learned, learned again, and reinforced in some vastly different companies and over a span of decades. It occurs to me that the lessons I felt important to put in the book, were all learned from experience. It was the experience gained from:

- doing it wrong until the correct way was found
- observing up close the critical errors of others around me, and learning what not to do
- my managers and superiors guiding me when I was about to go off track and sometimes suggesting ways to proceed

- seeing people who worked for me solving problems/issues at hand and learning from that experience
- learning from a crisis - which can energize and get the creative juices flowing
- experimenting continually trying to find out what worked
- finally, learning from customers, clients and other executives, and picking up ideas that worked

Notice that none of these methods were learned by reading "how to books." So, don't consider the lessons in this book to serve as a "how to" or "recipes" for you to use. The objective of the lessons is to stimulate your thinking on how, or whether, some ideas or techniques mentioned here might fit your business situation - maybe with some modification. Maybe they will bring to mind a better way – a new lesson.

So enjoy my journey and my lessons and see what fits.

Lesson 1: Preparation – Notebooks
In early 1978, I accepted my first job inside a plant. As a NAS product manager, for a line of plug compatible IBM mainframe products, I was required to interface with engineering, manufacturing, strategic marketing, sales and customers. The amount of information coming at

me each day was overwhelming. The GM of the operation to whom I reported, strongly suggested that I would need to document daily the important details, decisions and issues, if I were to be able to follow up on the myriad of tasks ahead, and have a good reference book to assure my success.

So, I have kept notebooks every day of my business life since 1978. Each page may be filled with people I have met, subjects discussed, decisions made, technical drawings, action items or just about any graphic that I thought was worthy of noting. I have referred to those manuals in writing this one. A couple of illustrations here are examples of some random pages from notebooks. **See illustrations 3.1 and 3.2. (these actual pages were difficult to render clearly)**

From the notebook entries, I estimate that I have interfaced with over 1,000 industry executives – not counting ones from the companies I was working with at the time. These meetings included person to person and teleconference meetings, and took place in all of the countries mentioned in the chapter on, *Background – A company by Company Overview.*

An interesting note: While reviewing my notebooks in writing this book, I discovered I had a meeting with executives from a mainframe database company that had recently been purchased by Intel. The founding executives were still in place though. They had come to NAS looking for a smaller, less expensive IBM compatible system to which they could port their database software. Their notion was to have that system be a back-end database system for IBM mainframes. This was in 1979. A meeting I had completely forgotten. No business deal occurred during these visits and subsequent ones. BUT, less than four years later, I was Intel's GM of that Austin, TX based database operation. I guess the point here is sometimes your industry may seem small – you will meet people again. Probably the reason for the saying, "don't burn your bridges."

I classified this first lesson as "Preparation", because the process of keeping important data for future retrieval and not trusting to memory or cryptic notes gives one an edge in every meeting. I was prepared to "pick up where we left off", and to report on my action items and remind others of theirs.

Preparation – Lesson 2: Objectives & Key Results
This key part of preparation dovetails nicely with the notebook part of preparation. Remember, after leaving NAS, I went to Intel and picked up one of the most important ingredients of preparation – the culture of utilizing objectives and key results.

The Intel culture at the time, under President Andy Grove, included strict adherence to a process where every Intel employee was required to create a set of 4-6 objectives each quarter. Under each objective were the key results (steps) that must be accomplished to meet that objective. Each objective must be quantitatively measurable – exactly what was to be accomplished, exactly when it was to be accomplished. The same was true for the key results. These Objectives and Key Results were reviewed by the employee and his manager each month and at the end of the quarter they were graded by both. A miss of an objective of even a day was graded as a complete miss and received a zero grade on the objective.

I put this down as a lesson on preparation, because I could so clearly see what they prepared the manager and employee to accomplish. They also had the effect of preparing an employee to "manage himself". He was prepared, and knew what was expected of him.

I felt much of the Intel culture at the time was extremely effective at getting the most from each employee. **Intel defined culture as what employees do when no one is watching.** It worked and seemed to empower people because they were managing themselves. It matched with another tenet of the Intel culture that stressed moving the decision making to the lowest level possible.

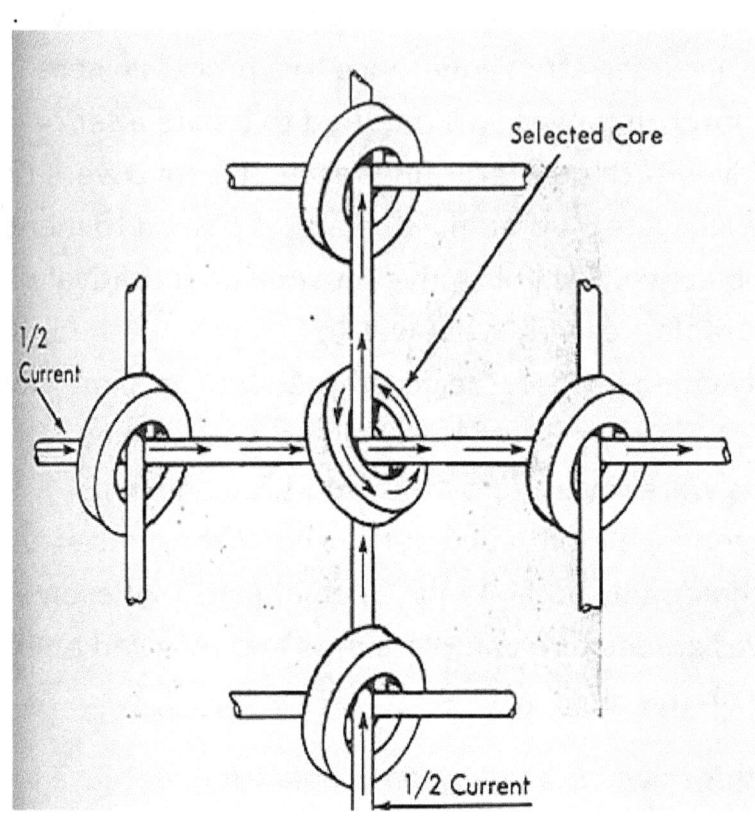

Illustration of computer core memory
Used in computers in 1960's - 1975

4 PERSONAL LESSONS
LESSONS 3 & 4:

I have mentioned it before, but its importance bears repeating.

Lesson 3: Know what your priorities are. Write them down. Refer to them at least once a year to see if you are true to your priorities.

We get busy in our business careers. It is not always clear if we are just *going along* or if we still have our focus on our priorities. Mine were:

1. Are you learning anything? This was important for me. I felt if I continued to learn more about what would be required to "round me out" in my industry, then I would be prepared to take on larger roles and more responsibility. I was aiming for broad experience from systems engineering to General Management and President.

2. Are you having any fun? I can't stress this one enough. Work can be tedious, exhausting, and stressful. Worse though if it becomes boring and uninteresting. So, if you are having fun at work – then it's not boring or as stressful because you find it fun. I would have to say, looking back on my 50 years in business; I had a lot of fun, enjoyment and satisfaction. I considered it a blast! I guess things look better in the rear view mirror.

3. Are you making any money? As you notice, making money was not the top of my list – only made number 3. Many times I felt I could have persevered and stayed in jobs that were not fulfilling my priorities one and two, but were more plentiful on the monetary side. The fun and learning something were more important to me. The best case I can use to illustrate this is my job at Intel. I was making money and (as it turns out), getting generous stock options that should have kept me there- as they were designed to do. But I thought I saw more of that motivating "fun" somewhere else.

You will have to establish your own priorities. You may come up with an entirely different set. But remember, they must be chosen to last a business lifetime. Of course they could be changed. But I never changed mine.

Lesson 4: Don't Forget Ethics/Morality/Trust. I put these under one lesson because I see them closely related.

Since I started my career more than 50 years ago, it seems like business was more ethical then, than now. So, maybe this lesson is even more important today and going forward. If you set your boundaries on these qualities early and keep them, then no one should be able to give you "excuses" for violating them. I believe you will earn respect from some who would have you forget your ethics/morality, and you may even cause a change in theirs.

In my business life, we mostly trusted our business leaders and our political leaders. Is this still true today? Not as much I think.

How did I learn lessons on these? Thankfully, I learned from observing breakdowns of these qualities in others around me. Raised in the

Midwest, I think I came with a set of values like "my word is my bond", and the golden rule.

What were some of the violations of these qualities I observed first hand? **Well, remembering that moral behavior at work means not getting "too friendly" with co-workers.** There were other sayings like – "don't get bred where you earn your bread', and "don't dip your pen in the company ink". I am sure there are many more similar sayings. They are all true. Here is the lesson. It is always found out. I saw this at IBM, and Intel. These were two stellar companies by almost any measure. But when someone gets in a position of power then it seems that the morality side of the brain may turn off. In multiple cases, people were either fired or reassigned. That's a big price to pay in one's career.

Here's a true story. As a rather new salesman in IBM (remember I was an S.E. for years before moving into sales), I was assigned a small account from another sales rep. The lady that ran the business could only see me after business hours (quite a bit after business hours) because of her business schedule. It was my first call on her one winter evening. We discussed how additional IBM solutions (of course hardware and software) might benefit her business. She appeared interested, and finally said to me, "do you really want my business". "Certainly, I said if it would improve your operation". Then she told me what it would take to get her to sign on the dotted line. When I heard that, I immediately thought that IBM was testing me with this situation and trying to see if I would fall into this trap. Were there hidden microphones or cameras?

Well I did what I knew to do and "was a good boy" and by the way, didn't get the order. But it did teach me that this sort of thing does happen.

Ethics and Trust to me is basically doing business honestly. We have all heard of the philosophy of "win, win". This is where both sides feel that they have gained something in the deal. I really mean more than that though.

There have been so many examples of breaks in trust and ethics I observed that I thought I would only give a few to illustrate.

When is an agreement an agreement? Most would agree that it is when both parties have agreed to the terms of the agreement and have signed and dated their agreement. Apparently this is not so for some. I worked for a company (not named here) that encouraged me as the Director of OEM sales to draft some initial business objectives for a partnership with our largest OEM customer. This customer was a large, profitable and growing company. The customer shared a lot of their business plans and strategies with us and we did with them.

They agreed to the conditions of the agreement outline and a complete Agreement was prepared. I delivered it for them to sign which they did. Returning to my HQ, the management signed and faxed the agreement back to the OEM customer. It was received by fax. But just after that, my company management had been apparently been talked out of it by a board member and sent a fax negating the Agreement. Now, I believe that almost any Agreement can be changed, re-negotiated or even cancelled, but not without facing the customer with why and certainly not by fax with no explanation. The OEM customer was angry and the tale of unethical behavior spread through this small segment of the industry within a few days. The lesson here is that unethical behavior can't be kept a secret.

When is pay yourself first fraud? In another large software company I worked for, there was an SEC investigation of revenue fraud. Cooking the books would be a good term for this misstep. Revenue from a forward quarter was moved into a current quarter in order to allow four key managers to pay themselves a bonus of $1.1 billion on false revenue performance for the current quarter. Maybe it was a little too large not to be noticed. They should have remembered the old saying - **greed will bury even the lucky eventually.**

Working with a company I co-founded in China I saw many examples of questionable ethics. Everyone is familiar with the problem of stealing of intellectual property that China is famous for, and this happened to our company too. **But the example I want to point out is one of Trust.**

Two of us started the China Company, which also included a U.S. company and a Hong Kong company. Co-founders were me, and my friend, a Chinese American. Our first major customer was a U.S. security company that wanted a second source for a network security device and improvements in its cost and quality. I introduced us to this company because of my long-time friendship with their company CEO and Chairman, whom I had worked for at Intel. After he left Intel, I became the GM of his Intel systems operation. We knew each other, had worked together, and as a consequence trusted one another.

So, when I said our engineers and manufacturing folks in China could provide lower cost and higher quality devices (both hardware and software), he gave us the opportunity. We performed well and they quickly became our largest customer and gave us additional work.

So, in the first case we got the business because the CEO knew me and trusted me. However sometime during the second year, my Chinese co-founder made a mistake of angering the wrong manager at the security company and it looked like we might lose their business. I called on the CEO to explain what the misunderstanding was. Since the Chinese co-founder spoke English as a second language there could be margin for misunderstanding and "here is what he really meant to convey". What I said was true and since the trust had been established over years, the incident was forgiven and business continued.

The lesson about morality, ethics and trust should be obvious. They are not. Some of the best and brightest I knew committed errors in judgment. We see it every day almost, by those with power in government and business. So, while it may seem obvious, you need to guard against straying on these qualities. Violations can end careers.

If you build your career on trust, and honesty even when it may be easier to let them slide a bit – then you will be trusted.

5 *SALES & SALES MANAGEMENT* LESSONS 5,6 &7:

Lesson 5: Salesman Lesson: There have been so many good books and classes on effective selling, that I thought I would not go into that topic except for just two lessons – counselor selling and the CAPS report as a selling tool. Many times salesmen get a bad rap. Sometimes they deserve it though. To get so caught up in pushing a product instead of solving customer issues, can earn that bad rap very quickly.

In the early '60's when I joined IBM as a systems engineer, they had a reputation of being honest, **"counselors",** that could be depended on to make certain the customer was getting good advice on what the systems would do and how they could best be used. Of course, the good 'ole systems engineer was there to make certain all went well. In those days, an S.E., or even more than one, was assigned to accounts to design applications for systems and actually code in many cases. All this was done to ensure the customer's success. Some good friendships were made and some lasting careers were assured for the competent IT managers who knew they count on their IBM salesman to get them their next job if necessary. A popular phrase in those days, if you want a safe decision – "order IBM."

The term counselor selling began to be the "tag" that IBM wanted its salesmen to be known for. It was the emphasis of IBM industry training. IBM did an excellent job of training salesmen and S.E.s for the industries in which they worked – banking, manufacturing, distribution, medical, government etc. This industry training together with the training on hardware systems and software gave the salesman a legitimate claim to "counselor salesman".

So the lesson here is to position yourself as a counselor (salesman) in the eyes of your customer. This means not only knowing your product, but how it is used in similar companies to his and what benefits were achieved by other clients.

I had an opportunity to teach IBM sales school. I won't get into all of the sales techniques we tried to instill in our students, but there was great emphasis on how and if the salesman could identify with the industry issues and specific issues of this customer. Empathize. If you were to help this client in his business ask – What would he like to improve in his present systems? Where would it be important to save time? What could help reduce his risk? What could increase his revenue? What would help improve quality? Questions like this get you and the client in "solution mode."

Don't assume you have the solution in your pocket ready to spring on your client, but let the "counselor interview" determine if you even have one.

Using these questions and genuinely identifying with the desires of a client proved to me their effectiveness in getting both client and salesman what they desired – a solution and an order.

I was out on calls with a new sales trainee in Decision Data, the company I joined after leaving IBM. We made our first ever call on a large bank. I had no idea if we had a product or service that would help this client and told him so as we walked in the door. But if we could have just a few minutes to discuss his operation we could both determine if we needed to proceed.

To cut to the net of the story, by questioning/interviewing this client he revealed that he was having difficulty getting monthly reports out in time for his management. This was becoming a problem for his management and then obviously for him. What was the bottleneck? He did not have enough print capacity to do all of the printing required even though he felt he had the computing power. What if we could put in another compatible printer with twice the speed of his current printers? "Yes that could be a great help." Then of course we did have a solution – a great new printer that would give him what he needed – **less headache for him from his management each month.**

A one-call sale by the way.

The salesman's hammer Another story that is quite dated now, but still represents creative salesmanship, concerns the Pittsburgh Plate Glass salesman, Charlie. PPG had just come out with a new auto safety glass that would not shatter into dangerous shards of glass when broken. Instead the shattered glass formed harmless beads of glass. The company salesmen were armed with sales tools describing all of the technical reasons behind the new glass – the materials, the process of manufacturing etc.

But there was one salesman in the company whose sales numbers were far above all others – Charlie. Charlie's management called him into HQ one day and said, "Charlie you are the most productive salesman we have and we'd like to know what your secret is." "What do you say to your prospects?"

Charlie said, "Well I carry in a big hammer and hold the glass then I hit it." His management thought that was a great way to illustrate the benefits of the new safety glass, and had Charlie do his demo at the upcoming national sales meeting. In the following months, sure enough, every territory showed increased sales. However, Charlie's sales were even greater than before and still the highest.

Management called Charlie to HQ again, and asked what he had changed to still be out selling the entire staff. Charlie explained that he indeed was doing something different now. What is it?

Charlie said, "This time I give the prospect the hammer, and I hold the glass."

Lesson 6: The Customer Annual Progress Summary (CAPS).
I learned this lesson while at IBM, but used it throughout my career. It is a powerful tool to put the salesman and the customer on the same wave length and effectively reinforces the counselor selling concept. The IT department or MIS department, whichever nomenclature you prefer, is a key engine of today's businesses. In many companies its effective use and growing capability is key to the success of an enterprise. So this CAPS presentation that the salesman requests of his customer's upper management, in most cases will be

welcomed.

Here's how it works. Once per year the salesman prepares a presentation for the upper management of his customer. The purpose is to review the successes and areas to improve, and to interactively outline with management during the presentation, the course for the next year. Sound like you are part of the customer's team?

If the customer has prepared a Strategic Long Rang Plan, then this presentation should tie into it. In many IT installations, the IBM team would hold a several-day planning session with key customer management to create and/or update the plan. And of course, part of that plan dealt with the solutions to be supplied from the IT department.

Prior to preparing the CAPS report, the salesman would discuss it and its purpose with the IT management. No surprises here.

What's in it? As an example, my IBM CAPS presentation included:

- Days of customer education that IBM supplied for IT people
- Days of customer executive education

- New installations with the reminder of what mission(s) it was to serve (i.e. support more on-line users, create better response time to users etc.)
- New applications that successfully went live
- Possibly some suggestions of examples of benefits like cost savings or reduction of risk or gain of competitive edge
- All of the positive achievements worthy of note
- Things that need improvement then could lead into……name the benefits.
- Now the portion to generate direction for the next year which might include – next steps in hardware or software implementation, additional education for IT personnel and executives, examples of other users in this industry who have benefitted from applications not currently on this customers system, and possible new systems or applications now becoming available (note that this is not the prime reason for the presentation)
- This part should be interactive and allow for some definition and agreement on the IT plans for next year.

I have found this tool to be one of the most effective tools a salesman can use to put himself into the role of counselor. In other cases, through the many years after the IBM experience, I was still using it. In other companies, I found that the CAPS was virtually unheard of and not used.

It works outside of IBM and with products much different than IBM or other computer technology related products. It proved very effective in working with the management of a large OEM in the company I co-founded, HierStar. In that example it served to update management on how the quality of an OEM device was being improved. It further offered a great opportunity to make suggestions for additional improvement. It also offers a face to face discussion that can cause creativity to flow for plans for the next year.

Lesson 7: Sales Management

There are so many good suggestions I am tempted to put in this lesson, but I have only put in one lesson that really worked well for me across many companies.

If you are a manager of salesmen you know you have to hire, train, fire, promote and motivate. But your management expects a sales forecast from you. They would like it accurate as possible in order to plan inventory, manufacturing etc.

The sales funnel. I have found the sales funnel to be extremely helpful in getting the best forecast information from a sales force. It breaks down the process from initial call to order and each step along the way. (see illustration 5.1)

Here are the five steps:

1. Understand if the prospect is qualified to buy now,

2. Present your product/service and get feedback, (benefits emphasized)

3. References to achieve prospect conviction (I agree that could provide me ...),

4. Find the urgency on the prospects part (busy season coming up, or slow season, or end of year or new products coming on line etc.)

5. Close – ask for the order in order to meet the urgency found above

Questioning salesmen on which step they are realistically in, and what it will take to move to the next step will give a better idea of how far away the order may be.

To use this funnel effectively, it will take some sales training on the steps in the sales process. You must factor in for your industry – the length of the average sales process from start to order, and the number of active prospects that can be in the funnel at any one time.

6 PRODUCT MGMT., GM, PRES/CEO LESSONS 8-13:

In this chapter we will deal with some of the key functions of a product manager, general manager and/or CEO. If we don't get these functions mostly right we may not have a product to manage or a business to run. These stories from the past provide real life examples that might help to prove that statement.

Lesson 8: Product Announcement Timing

Do you remember the Osborne computer company? It introduced an early personal computer called the Osborne 1. With extremely poor timing the company introduced the Osborne 2 well before it was ready to ship. What do you think the customers and prospects did? They stopped ordering Osborne 1's, and instead decided to wait for the future delivery of the Osborne 2. For a new, growing company, that shut down of the revenue stream of waiting customers, was enough to cause the company to fail.

Interestingly, this failure in planning new product introduction has been repeated many times since the Osborne experience.

I dealt with this announcement timing issue on several product introductions and re-introductions over the years in my experience.

We were particularly sensitive to the timing of new product introduction at NAS. The job was to make our introductions sensitive to the sales curve, or life cycle curve, of the product being replaced. Obviously, there is not always a product being replaced, so the next lesson on new product introduction positioning would apply.

 Objectives – time the replacement product introduction as the demand curve for the existing product is falling off. Not too soon. Not too late. This is not as straight forward as you may think. Considerations are, maintaining revenue, manufacturing ramp up, parts in inventory of the old product, competition announcements, sales and marketing launch materials and dates etc. It was somewhere in this time frame that I became aware of customer focus groups as a way of "proving" the need for the new product and how it might be received.

At Intel, a first introduction of the solid state disk product was a disaster. The product was introduced with great fanfare to an audience of the largest IBM mainframe users (including IBM labs and factories). The first installation was at a Texaco site. It did not live up to the hype and failed to perform as advertised. This negative publicity was in all of the trade rags.

Now what do you do? Well, we went back to the drawing board. Re-engineered the memory mapping for replacement memory and came up with our "bullet proof" idea mentioned below. The products were re-logoed and had different packaging and look. A family of two products now replaced the old product. Several willing customers were recruited to quietly install and run the new machines until we were certain that they were solid in the demanding customer environment. With discounts as a reward, those new install sites were now reference sites. And away the product went!

Lesson 9: Positioning and Messaging
New products need to be positioned with the correct messaging for their introduction. One definition is:
A marketing strategy that aims to make your product occupy a distinct position, relative to competing brands, <u>in the mind of the customer</u>. Companies apply this strategy either by emphasizing the distinguishing features of their brand (what it is, what it does and how,

etc.) or they may try to create a suitable image (inexpensive or premium, utilitarian or luxurious, entry-level or high-end, etc.).

There are many positioning examples of companies announcing new products. In Intel, we announced our new solid state disk product with the distinguishing feature of being "bullet proof". (Remember the product was attached to IBM mainframe channels as a vital performance peripheral that couldn't go down). In the case of our product, it was composed of non-volatile memory; therefore it had no moving parts. It featured on-board spares that would automatically be configured to take the place of any memory failures. The success of this product family appears to validate its correct positioning or messaging statement against competition. At the time, this product was unique in having that feature.

The most important point is positioning is to develop messaging that sharply defines a customer's view of a product or service compared to its competition. This concept of positioning from my experience may be the key to opening up a venture capital firm's purse. I have made several product presentations to VCs where it seemed positioning my product correctly (at least in their mind) against alternative competitor products or against the customer deciding to do nothing was paramount.

Some good questions to test your positioning could be - Who needs it? Why yours against the existing choices? How will you command the price(s) you are proposing? How will you get your product to market versus your competitors? Do you have sustainable differentiation? Does your product have barriers to a competitor's entry into your space?

Once you have positioned your product, it is difficult to change it. Remember it has already been established in the mind of your customers and prospects.

Lesson 10: Engineers, Bless Them
It seems to be important in working with engineers as a GM, that you must ask questions – constantly – all of the time – in an attempt to get to the root of the issue. Products may fail, and new products are sometimes not inventive enough.

Two lessons I learned:

1. Engineers will tell a GM what they think he wants to hear, and

2. Engineers have a tendency to suggest what they

know how to do, rather than take some risk beyond their comfort zone.

This does not mean they are not good engineers, but just risk adverse. Unfortunately, many engineers (some of your competitor's engineering teams maybe), are not so risk adverse and willing to try on new approaches. Your company and products may be competing against those engineers.

If you have seen the recent movie, *Jobs*, you saw Steve Jobs constantly question and challenge his technical folks. He seemed to use questions to get them thinking, and being more creative. He did shake up the troops and got a unique product space (re: positioning) for Apple's products.

Lesson 11: Product Forecasting Lessons

Salesmen and sales managers get annoyed with the task of regular forecasts. It is hard enough for existing products with some track record, but for new products – well it can be a real challenge. In this section on forecasting lessons, I have put in some examples from my experience that prove the value of accurate product forecasting.

This section is not a treatise on how to forecast. There are many tactics and processes already described in the annals of business education that perform that instruction. What is discussed here is the result of poorly executed product forecasting. Once you have lived through the consequences of these mistakes, you will not soon forget their lessons.

What goes into forecasting?
One thing for sure is your competition. How does your product or service compare?

- Existing product or new product?
- Do you have any feature advantages that competition does not?
- How does your price compare to competition? Room for price reductions?
- Performance on key performance measures against you competition?
- Your positioning and messaging – is it sharply defined in customers mind?
- Quality of your product or service versus your competition?
- Are you closely monitoring your competition and what they are likely to do about your price, new announcements etc.?
- Do you have a defendable niche product?
- What did you learn from previous forecasts?

One thing I learned is that you need to understand what a missed forecast can mean.

Remember the IBM S/370 announcements mentioned earlier? If you have delivery dates of almost three years like they did, how can you assure you won't lose customers who won't wait that long?

In the IBM case, they used a strategy of interim systems upgrades to allow an increase in a customer's computing power until their S/370 could be delivered. Of course, the customer order response was extremely under forecasted. Maybe a manufacturing issue too. Without some program like the "interim system" strategy, IBM could have demonstrated the "Osborne effect", and the revenue stream might have dried up. IBM escaped that effect thanks more to hungry salesmen that had to sell something to get paid and satisfy their customers need for more computing power. It also helped that many customers were coming from the S/360 base, which probably made a move to competition less likely. Maybe no other systems vendor at the time could have gotten away with this strategy.

The Itel example has already been briefly discussed. Here is how they forecasted. They looked at how much revenue growth they wanted year to year and forecasted the number of systems that would produce that number. No regard to their primary competition (IBM) and what they were likely to do. Remember an earlier statement in this book; IBM assesses how many losses they are willing to take from competitors and when their threshold is reached, they act. React they did. They announced the Systems 4300 family – a whole new price/performance equation. Shouldn't Itel have suspected this announcement? As a matter of fact they did and so did their supplier, NAS. Go figure. As you have already read, this miss on a forecast killed a company in just a few months.

Other examples I have seen included a systems forecast one year at Intel. Recall that Intel Systems Division was in the data server business with Unix-based networked servers. One year a very optimistic GM forecasted a large increase in the number of servers. Of course, that required manufacturing to order parts and begin ramping to satisfy the forecast. It was a disaster. Only about 25% of the forecast resulted in actual sales and subsequent builds and shipments. The biggest disaster was a huge parts and semi-finished goods inventory that became essentially useless. I saw this problem up close because I was asked to run that operation the next year. My biggest challenge was product cost as I had to "eat" the unusable parts in inventory. A rather creative education discount and/or donation program was launched to entice colleges and universities to take most of that inventory off our hands. And Intel got a tax credit for the donations. Thank goodness for creative accounting folks that can help a

GM.

In addition to the "What goes into a forecast" questions above, I learned to importance of prospect interviews and focus groups.

Focus groups are probably familiar, but interview techniques are probably not. I am not against typical surveys, but the data from surveys can be misleading. Were the survey questions appropriate? Did the prospect understand each question? What would they really have revealed if a dialog between prospect and interviewer had occurred? Interviewing, if done correctly, can reveal the desires, the concerns and the risks a client feels – and that is important. Phone interviewing, to a selective, and wider audience can provide more prospect input than focus groups. The key to effective use of this technique is the expertise of the interviewer. He must know the subject well and be an effective listener.

Both the focus and interview approaches should produce valuable forecast input on new products.

Lesson 12: Importance of Quality
Everyone should agree, that a product's quality or lack thereof will be revealed very quickly in the field of use. Your customer will tell you.

Can quality bring a higher price? Consider the example of the re-engineered solid state disk products at Intel mentioned earlier. Re-engineering accomplished a quality feature that could be easily translated to a benefit by the typical large systems customer. More users on line with better response time was really the feature. But the benefit came from not having to answer all of those user calls that would come in if a system or key component was down. And those calls could come in late at night, on weekends etc. What a way to live, so – "I'll take the bullet proof disk with no moving parts and on-board spares", was the response of many prospects.

Lesson 13: Find the Golden Keys

I found it very useful as a GM to find the 5-6 golden keys to the success of an operation I was running. I had P&L responsibility, so things that affected the bottom line were critical. That was the principle measure of your success as a GM. But there were so many. **How do you select the 5-6 most key items– or golden keys.**

What affects revenue and profit?

1. At the revenue line it is likely sales velocity, returns, forecasts, promotions etc.

Also, consider price and pricing policy – consider discounts, whether you lease or purchase your products.

2. COGS, or cost of goods sold has a direct effect on the bottom line. Remember the bloated inventory inherited from the missed forecast I mentioned that I was asked to handle at Intel? Result was a bloated COGS.

3. Personnel and personnel motivation

4. Research and development. This line can grow quickly with new products to develop.

5. Manufacturing ramp and per cent content from your company (parts, packaging etc.)

6. Quality will be a part of manufacturing and engineering cost, but quality failures in the field have a potentially very large remedy cost.

It seems so obvious. Just follow down your P&L statement. The important factor after picking your 5-6 golden keys is how will you measure them on a regular basis, and how will they point out, in reports you design, that something needs your attention.

Sometimes I was faced with too high cost of goods (example of the huge inventory due to unsold product).

Sometimes I found carrying leases internally (on our books as leases) on high-priced products was limiting the revenue that could be recognized.

In COGS, how much was our content and how much did we have to procure from outside. Could that be changed?

Research and development projects if unmanaged would lead to more folks and more projects – maybe not all contributing to revenue in the same way, and not consistent with strategy.

Good people, of course, are key to sales, and product success. How do I determine if the turnover is too high and if we are losing too many key people?

The manufacturing ramp I found to be a very important item too. Uneven demands on manufacturing for production of product, has consequences in higher cost and potentially lower quality. I wanted a steady state ramp in manufacturing – no sharp ups and/or downs.

So for my golden keys, I needed daily or weekly reports. I knew what the numbers were that I wanted to see reported – that is, what success must look like.

If any of the golden keys elements of success were falling short what do you do?

At least you have determined where you need to dive down deeper to understand the missed numbers.

For example in the case of lower revenue on the expensive Intel products that had Intel carrying the leases – something had to be changed. I had experience with leasing companies in other jobs. Upon investigation, we found we could sell leases to one of those companies and take more revenue up front.

COGS that are too high according to your model objective, will take some investigation. In some cases, I found opportunities for increasing our content in the product bill of material which helped reduce cost. In other cases, some re-engineering would allow less expensive manufacturing and parts costs.

Sometimes the objective of lower parts and manufacturing costs may not be well thought out. One OEM customer of a network security product we were engineering and manufacturing for them, decided on a new design for the packaging. They gave that design project to another company, and then we were supposed to perform the manufacturing engineering to build the product with lower cost and higher quality. It was obvious to us after a little study there was no way these goals could be achieved. With our best talent analyzing the packaging design we knew that both cost savings and quality improvement could not be achieved – not by us nor any other company. We were determined to keep this customer happy so we took our best shot(s) at achieving the goals. However, here is where the CAPS presentations really came to the rescue. We made our case to executive management. Yes they had a "cute" design. But their goals could not be met, so we proposed more effective solutions without directly "killing their baby".

Quality is a part of engineering and manufacturing costs. Design-in quality in the product, and test for quality in the manufacturing process. A lesson I learned on this point was expensive. This case involves a small network security device we were making. Once you seal a products package, and it cannot be opened without destroying the electronics inside, you better have a lot of quality checks before it goes out the door. And if you have shipped the devices (hardware, software and firmware), and they fail in the field, then you will get it back – returns. And you have to re-supply at your expense. This is an expensive lesson to learn. So whatever your reports are for understanding daily quality, a GM and CEO must be alert on this one.

The point is made. Selecting your golden keys is

essential. Monitoring them, even if requires daily monitoring, could be the difference between profit or loss. But it will require digging in or diving down. Making the issue visible allows creative thinking to come up with solutions, and they need to come as soon as possible.

Last point Once you establish your golden keys and the methods of reporting on them, you can establish this culture with your employees. It will clarify in their minds what is important. The job of monitoring and fixing issues gets easier with more "hands on deck." If you have implemented the Objectives and Key Results, concept for all employees, then their role in monitoring can fit nicely into their work responsibility.

ARRAY OF WORKSTATIONS & LAPTOP

7 STRATEGY & LONG RANGE PLANNING
LESSONS 14 - 17

Lesson 14: Pricing Strategy

We probably wouldn't need much strategy if there were – no competitors. But alas, if we have found a market for our product and/or service and if we can make a profit from filling that market demand, then we will find company (competition).

Strategy covers a lot of ground in a growing business.

- Product strategy – what product(s)
- Pricing strategy
- Marketing or Merchandising strategy including positioning strategy
- Strategy of identifying our best defensible niche
- Product introduction strategy
- Product add-ons and product spin offs
- Product end of life strategy

- Acquisition or merger strategy
- For small or startup companies – an exit strategy
- Executive succession plan

Every one of these has been a part of my experience somewhere along the way. So, maybe a few lessons came out of that experience that could be useful to others.

Pricing Strategy is a key part of forming strategies for an operation. What do you do? You first look at your costs and margin requirements to determine if you can make a profit at various realistic planned sales volumes. From my early days with IBM teaching the financial side of an IT decision, I developed a short hand P&L format that I used many times over the years. By plugging in sales, cost of goods sold, R&D, and SG&A (sales and general and administrative expenses), one could quickly arrive at Net Profit Before Taxes (NPBT). It became useful in measuring the expense lines of a P&L in a pro-forma way. Usually, for a specific business or operation, the expense lines as a per cent of sales were key measuring items toward a successful business operation. For example, it is probably well known in your company what R&D is as a percentage of sales….and so on. Nothing startlingly magic about this, but I found it useful so many times in planning go or no go product decisions etc.

It is of course important to see what the competition is pricing for similar products or services. If you had to meet competitions pricing – would you still make a profit? If you had to beat competitions pricing – would you still make a profit? Can your product(s) demand a higher price because of additional useful features compared to the competition? What will your competition likely do in response to your pricing?

You may only have a business, with your set of products, if you have considered these questions - and still see profit ahead.

Selling at Less than Cost
Here is a pricing strategy that makes little sense on the surface, but wait there's more. Here is an example of what I mean. At one time in my Intel career, I was asked to take over as GM of Value Added System operation. This was an operation that had never made a profit in its several-year existence. At hand was a bid from the Army that we were preparing for our reply. From looking at what our cost was, (this is the operation that was caught with excess inventory of parts because of a badly missed forecast the previous year), it did not appear we could be competitive.

The Controller Rides to the Rescue
It was agreed between me and the controller for the VAS operation, that If we wanted to win this bid we

needed to be very creative. This bid was a request for systems and software over a six year period and with a small number of initial shipments to begin not for several months. Then volumes would gradually increase.

We had to solve two problems to have a chance with this bid.

1. Get rid of some of the excess inventory of parts that were outdated and couldn't be used in this bid.
2. Even after executing on number 1., we needed to supply a lower price to be competitive.

Solution to number 1 required donations to educational institutions, and universities that would accept free systems and a lot of semi finished goods. A program was started to do this and it took off rapidly. Intel, of course, got the tax break deductions of these donations. This reduced the inventories significantly and sharply reduced our cost of goods for new products. We didn't have the carrying cost of the old inventory. This was of significant help.

Solution to number 2 required a sharp pencil on product cost. Remember we did not have to deliver many systems in the first months of the contract. The cost curve on parts was continually moving down on our product content of the products. After taking another look at the shipment ramp and the cost reduction ramp we expected, we could afford to price at prices that lost money initially, but got very profitable inside the same fiscal year.

And that's exactly what we did. We won the Army contract and the operation became profitable for the first time – all in less than one year.

The lesson I learned on pricing was to always consider that in the computer industry, the product cost treadmill is continually moving to lower pricing for same capability. Memory prices serves as a good example of that cost-lowering treadmill.

Lesson 15: Product Add-ons and Spin offs

Generally, with each product introduction there is a plan for "mid life kickers", or add-on features and/or price reductions to prolong the product life cycle. In my experience planning for these add-ons is strategic, because it can prolong revenue and margins that help to offset continuing engineering and research expenses.

Product add-ons examples are plentiful in the computer industry. Itel, the large mainframe reseller used to claim that the large extra space in a mainframe cabinet (compared to IBM's jammed full cabinets), represented where the upgrades would go – extra memory, peripheral interfaces and additional processing boards.

Interestingly, this was an effective "pitch" to prospective customers. The typical IBM customer was used to upgrades requiring two trucks – one to remove the old system and one to bring in the new system. Upgrades like this were extremely disruptive to an IT department, and could result in costly downtime for the operation. So, the **upgrade in place concept** offered by the new architecture IBM plug compatible vendor was very appealing.

The Itel example is just one example that has been used many times in industry. Many software upgrades to achieve enhanced performance are already in the base level software and just require a key to produce the performance upgrade for a customer. This comes at an additional price to the customer with no additional cost to the vendor. Good business.

So the lesson here on add-ons is to plan the one or more mid-life kickers in a product life cycle to keep revenue and margin alive for longer periods.

Spin offs are another interesting part of product planning. The question is what can the engineering investment made in the current product be used for in new products? The best example I can think of is another Intel example. The solid state disk product mentioned earlier required the development of a hardware and firmware interface to the channel controllers on an IBM or compatible mainframe.

That piece of engineering it was discovered could be used to produce a quite different product. The new product would solve the need for non-IBM devices to communicate to the IBM processor at channel speed. Up until that time these devices could only communicate at the speed of an IBM 3270 terminal (slow). This new capability opened up large, and previously untapped markets for these non-IBM devices and even included some IBM systems like the Series 1 computers, which also had the communication speed limitation problem. For that reason, IBM became one of the first customers for the product.

I have seen many examples of this spin-off product phenomenon since. There are examples of database products using the core technology to produce software for multiple machine operating systems and processors. In the area of security, there are examples from my experience where the base hardware and software was used to produce other similar products with additional features based on this proven base technology.

The motivation behind the examples I have experienced, was to **leverage previous engineering development**. It also allowed utilizing engineering that had the quality testing of previous products in the lab as well as the installed base.

There is no message here other than to use these opportunities for add-on and spin-offs in a product and life cycle plan.

Lesson 16: The Importance of a Skunk Works

A skunk works is a little different than the accepted notion of rapid prototyping.

Most companies in the Hi Tech industry, have already established the process of how products will be conceived and subsequently be developed. These companies have standard procedures of how they want the process to flow. Their process may include rapid prototyping but if so, they must still follow the process steps and it will take a while to get through the process flow. A process flow may go like this:

- Marketing develops **a marketing requirements document**. This document defines the market need, competition and requirements for a product to enter a specific market. It specifies the necessary cost to produce required margins. Also included, is the first customer ship date required for market entry and maximum profit potential.
- From the marketing requirements document, engineering produces their answer – **the engineer development plan**. It will include features, time

and cost for the product. There may be much iteration between engineering and marketing to arrive at compromises. Features may be dropped, added or changed. Dates may be later than requested and costs may be higher. Assuming there is a compromise agreement reached, then work begins and engineering tasks are scheduled.

Notice from this typical process flow, there is no testing of the new idea on customers and most of the time no prototype development to show prospective users.

In one company, even though there were standing orders not to have anything like a "skunk works" in my operation – we did it any way on a low-key basis. In this particular operation, we were building rather standard products (with competition from a lot of small and hungry companies), we were not really stretching the envelope. We had some software to run on these network servers that was uniquely ours, but that did not seem sufficient to establish – why our product.

Performance of the LAN based network servers was important and a key measurement for a customer. In order to address enhancing performance, it would take the process of requirement and engineering response months to complete. And large competitive bids were coming down in which we wanted to participate – and win.

So with this development in mind, the need for a skunk works that might prototype a future system emerged. What performance could be achieved by enhancing or upgrading the current system? At that time, our system (and most all others) had not produced a product that would support more than one processor board on the system's bus.

Then I remembered an old lesson. When selling the first small computer system as an IBM salesman, the customer surprised and amazed me with his question. Although the company was a small concern, and he was about to order an entry-level computer system he asked this question. "How far up the compatible IBM system family can I upgrade?" He would not be happy until we illustrated his potential upgrade path all the way up to System 360 model 70. That was up all of these upgrades – 360 model 30, model 40, model 50, model 60, model 62, and at that time the end of the line – 360 model 70. Did the customer ever upgrade to the upper models – no.

The lesson here is that the customer wants assurance that he will not outgrow his system – especially too soon. It can actually become a motivation to buy yours over the competition.

Remembering that lesson on upgradability, a couple of engineers were assigned the task of producing an upgrade path for our one board system product. This wasn't as easy as it seemed. The system bus interfacing to additional processor boards, was one part. But the operating system recognizing and utilizing an additional processor boards was a more difficult part.

What we really wanted was a prototype to demonstrate that upgrading to more processing power was real. Within weeks we had a running prototype and were able to demonstrate it as an illustration that we would be able to upgrade the base system if needed. The bid was won and the customer never needed to upgrade during the contract period to multiprocessor systems.

It may not always work this way, but without showing our lab prototype, we would never have convinced this prospect of our development path. Later on, multiple boards were supported – but much too late to have won this bid.

Introducing prototypes was also the key later on to winning at GM with prototype speech inspection stations that proved to be effective production products on the car production floor.

Lesson 17: Strategic Long-range Planning is something I found essential in setting the strategies to guide company execution. I was introduced to the importance of Strategic Long Range Planning while at IBM. I sat through several of these where outside IBMers were brought in to facilitate this process with some of our larger customers. A large bank in the south east was the first one I observed. The importance of an outsider, that is not one of the customer execs, was essential in providing a "neutral party" to the process. An insider executive would have the tendency to insert their viewpoints – and have the "power of the pen" or magic marker when capturing the group thoughts on an issue.

These planning sessions, usually ran from three full days to as much as five days. Later, I led these sessions for different industry clients.

Intel was very keen on having annual SLRP (Strategic Long Range Planning). Each operational group prepared and presented their five year plan to board-level executive management – who of course provided input and counsel to the presenter. Andy Grove was president at that time, and the key executive in the presentations. He was not at all bashful about commenting – "That's Bull Shit", when he felt you had not considered appropriate planning factors. He could always get you with his view of hinge factors. Risks and hinge factors were anything that could make your "wonderfully insightful plan" fall apart.

Such things as:

- Government actions that could have a negative effect
- Acts by competition that could have an effect
- People issues (he had to have some reasons to suspect this one)
- Product delays
- Unplanned market price pressure
- Probably many more that I didn't personally observe

Among the Intel GMs that I interfaced with, we used to count the Grove comments this way – add the number of "atta boys" and subtract the number of "dumb shits" to get your final Grove score. More "atta boys" and you were a "fair haired", "golden boy". So, I am proud to have received an atta boy note from Grove. It is included in the illustrations as Exhibit 7.1.

By the way, after the SLRP week of presentations, there was a company-wide SLRP dinner to honor the hours of work that had been required to put these plans together. The acronym SLRP when pronounced becomes – slurp dinner. I never will forget the look on my wife's face when I announced that I would be going to an Intel SLRP (slurp) dinner. I know what she must have imagined.

The SLRP Sets Your Annual Strategy

So, the lesson here on strategy is to use the assembled minds of your key execs to produce a SLRP that will address how you are going to meet you plan goals, and what strategies must be applied.

A general outline of a Strategic Long Range Plan

A SLRP in my experience follows the general outline below:

1. Define and fine tune the Mission of the business or operation, and write a **Mission Statement**.
2. **Define specific goals** that are directed at satisfying or achieving the Mission. These goal statements <u>must</u> be specific and measurable. It must clearly state what is to be achieved and when. A plan will include from 5 – 8 of these goal statements.
3. Under each goal statement, produce a set of **objectives that if met, will achieve the goal.** Again, each of these objectives will need to be defined with measurable achievements with their dates.
4. Next develop a set of **Key Results**. The objectives are measurable milestones toward achievement of a goal, and they require the steps or key results that must be achieved to satisfy the objective. Again, they must specific and measurable and specify the date of the step completion.

But remember

After a plan is agreed upon by the executive staff, stake it in. Resist the temptation to pull up the stakes and change it. Don't misunderstand, plans do change, but it should take a major event to cause that to happen. Obviously, an effective plan must be reviewed regularly to make sure the action steps are achieving the set objectives. Annually, this experience should be recalibrated, and the plan focus further sharpened. If managed correctly a SLRP will continue to focus the operations efforts on the objectives and goals, and not be too easily led to the "next target of opportunity".

8 DECISION MAKING
LESSONS 18 – 20:

Decision making is a very personal thing. It has a personality – yours. So in the lessons on decision making there is no attempt to make you change your personal style. However, noted here are some observations from experience that may add some additional perspective.

Lesson 18: Select your Trusted Team

Obvious right? Do you have one selected? Are you using them? Your team may not only those who work for you, and you have hired to be your "team", but the others in which you have confidence. And, it doesn't mean that the selected "team members" even realize they are on your virtual team. Searching out the best technical minds, financial minds, marketing minds and sales minds you have access to from current or even past companies you have worked with could be your team.

Sometimes you may only need counsel from the technical heads alone. Sometimes the marketing and technical heads will help with making your decisions. The lesson here is to realize that if you can put together your trusted team it can make your life easier. What you are looking for is input from different perspectives on the decision at hand – that you have to make.

And don't forget trusted customers. The right ones can give key input and perspective to your decision making process. Non disclosure agreements (NDA) are essential here. It should not be surprising that key customers like to be favored with being a part of decisions on new products, or even new sales and marketing policies – i.e. pricing or contract changes. The NDA protects you, and your trusted customer feels more like an insider.

What seemed to work best is when the "team members" felt like they were gaining from the relationship. Posing business or marketing questions to one of your techie team members could offer an alternative view and cause new questions to be asked and answered before decisions are made. I have seen customers express their interest in helping with decisions and they seem to get closer to the company and its products than ever before.

Lesson 19: Crisis may be your best teacher
You haven't really earned your leadership stripes until

you have managed through a crisis. I not suggesting that you go manufacture a crisis. Just wait – one will come when you least expect it. It may be a crisis caused by a quality glitch, competition, loss of key people, manufacturing issues or you name it. But it will demand your attention.

Another thing is for sure. It will test your thinking under fire. It will present your leadership image to those around you, and it will allow all of your team to "catch" your confidence.

Here are the main things a crisis will do for you.

- **It will make you goal focused – what is our business?**
- **It will bring out creativity in you and your team.**
- **It will allow an even stronger team to emerge on the other side of the crisis**

I have had what I would call a crisis, experiencing all of the issues mentioned above at one time or another. A good starting point is to ask this question.

What is the worst possible outcome? Then ask, what are the next most likely outcomes? This seems to put limits on the size of the problem or crisis. Now you can start damage control.

Next try to paint a more vivid picture of what a

solution(s) would look like. Maybe you will have several of these. Then generate a timetable for executing on the solutions. This is a time to show your calm during the crisis to your team. They look to you to determine if they should **"bale the water or abandon ship"**.

So the lesson here is, to take these simple ideas on steps to resolution of the crisis and manage through it. Take note of what works and what doesn't so you will be better next time. Remember, some people are hired just for their ability to think through the crisis steps when a company is in trouble. How do you think they got their expertise? They got it most likely from living through a number of "work outs" from past crises.

Lesson 20: Trust your Gut

One wants data to make decisions. Certainly, you want information, test results, competitive analysis, expert opinions and any data that would provide logic to your decision making process. But maybe our gut or intuition plays a significant role in our decision making too.

Once I heard the comment from a key executive that he wanted the data so he could justify the gut decisions he makes to his board.

In a recent Forbes article I read that, *"Our intuition accesses our accumulated experiences in a synthesized way so that we can make decisions and take action without any logical conscious consideration."*

When presented with the panoply of information you could search out in today's information utility, it is easy to get data overload. When is too much data inhibiting decision making? Is timely action important?

This process of data synthesizing seems to be what our intuition or gut does best. It certainly allows us to form judgments and take action in a more timely manner. Have you ever heard of "over thinking the problem", and consequently waiting too long to act? Or have you heard of the expression "analysis paralysis". One thing is for certain – if you never act you will never know for sure.

So with this lesson I am suggesting that if we have considered the data, and we have expertise in the area, then our intuition may be an excellent thing to listen to. I have had the instinct that a person or new position would not be right for me. But the data said something different, so I ignored by intuition. Most of the time my gut was right, and the logic was misleading.

So if our gut or intuition can be used in our decision making, how do we be sure it is not giving us wrong information? I guess I asked that question many times when wanting to "go with my gut" instinct.

I found my way of testing my gut decisions before I

acted, but not in a formal way. The above mentioned Forbes article by Campbell and Whitehead puts some process to that testing.

They suggest four tests before launching that gut decision.

1. The familiarity test: – thinking through past experiences for identical or similar experiences and decisions to see there are sufficient experiences to support sound judgment about the decision at hand.

2. The feedback test: - what was the feedback from past situations. Were the decisions perceived to be the right ones? Why? If not good feedback received– why?

3. The measured emotions test: - were there past experiences with traumatic results that may bias you from deciding in the same way? You may want to bring in others and solicit their opinions.

4. The independence test: - are you being influenced by inappropriate personal interests or attachments?

In my experience, I believe I performed many, or most, of these tests before making a gut decision. They are obviously good checks to include in your decision making when it is your gut or intuition that is being used.

Extra Lesson: The importance of "the Pause" in Decision Making

The experience of doing the work in a SLRP offers an opportunity that our action filled, information overloaded day does not. At time to reflect, to question, to contemplate and to include new insights, creativity and innovation in our plan. The planning session offers a respite from the "every day activity", to just pause - to step back.

............P.. a..u.. s ..e..........

For almost three decades I worked hard to show my drive, decisiveness and control of situations. It was important to me to show my ability to get things done. Then I discovered something. Even during a crisis, it is important to pause, to step back and question, involve others and seek out creative thinking from others. After all, it is the "others" we are attempting to develop into effective managers and leaders. If that is so, then a crisis becomes a great time to do some developing and to illustrate the - pause before acting culture.

Only recently, I discovered a book that covered that step back or pause before acting notion. It is called, *The Pause Principle (by Kevin Cashman).* It provides the research studies to prove the importance of developing a pausing-before-acting style of management. Although I was using the pause principle much of the time I was not aware that some of the world's key executives had discovered its importance and were using it too. My earlier tendency was to swift action. But I discovered later how much more effective it is to allow the space and time to question, synthesize, challenge time-held beliefs and allow those "Aha Moments" to enter.

Cashman's book pointed out that the world we work in is a high-speed, action oriented, fast changing and demanding one. It has shaped us. According to Cashman the world today is, Volatile; Unpredictable; Complex and Ambiguous. Amen to that. But that is the same one we must work in, and seek successful careers in too.

True story
I put this story under Gut feel, because sometimes it does talk to you and it may be important to listen.

Together with our European lawyer, I was negotiating a significant agreement and lots of money was at stake for both parties. Finally during several days of intense negotiation with the other company in London (all of their European execs were there), we reached a critical point – an impasse. The negotiation was stalled. There was a particular gentleman from Scotland who remained stubborn and unrelenting on some key business points on which we could not agree.

I remember thinking, how do I get out of this?

My legal person, who had been mostly quiet during the several days, abruptly put everything back in his brief case and stood up. He announced, "We're leaving, and if you still want to continue and finish this deal, you will meet us at our hotel in Paris but without the Scottish fellow".

We left. Sure enough, they met us at our hotel the next Monday without the Scot, and the agreement was finalized in just a few hours over dinner – which they bought.

I guess this lesson is "know when to hold 'em and know when to fold 'em", or bluff in this case.

So the lesson here comes to us from ancient tradition; withdraw and return; reflect and act. It's sound advice. To step back from the chaotic, frenzied present and maybe find wisdom, seems to be where effective leadership begins.

Even firemen who come to the crisis of a raging fire, first pause to consider if past solutions will work in this case, or will we have to try new methods.

Remember that a decision is only as good as the commitment behind it – get all your wood behind one arrow.

9 AGREEMENTS, CONTRACTS & NDAS
LESSONS 21 - 22:

Lesson 21: Agreement in Principle or MOU
The most important lesson I learned when working on unique agreements or contracts was to never allow the lawyers a first cut. There were so many agreements that were non-standard in my experience, making this point doubly important. Some were supplier to client, like the Intel to Memorex agreements.

Up until that point the lawyers always had taken the lead in preparing contracts. Bad idea. Generally the larger company controls the ball in that situation and their lawyers will draft the agreements. Of course, if you have been through this exercise you know that the draft is totally one-sided in favor of the lawyers company. There will be months of back and forth required to "fix" the agreement until it becomes a more balanced one.

Sometime, in the early 80's, I had the opportunity to contract with Memorex U.S. and later their European group for rather expensive products and their required spares and upgrades. There were lots of business details to be considered, including, price concessions for volume and field upgrades etc. The Memorex team I was negotiating with was led by an executive that introduced me to MOUs – Memorandum of Understanding agreements. (One is included as exhibit 9.1 at the end of this chapter). The purpose of the MOU, or sometimes called an Agreement in Principle, is to establish the business conditions and requirements of each party before the lawyers turn it into a formal agreement. The MOU is usually just a 2-3 page outline of the business details, prices and very importantly the completion date for the final agreement (got to give the two legal staffs a due date).

When the points in the MOU were agreed to by the business parties it was signed and became the marching orders for both sides to continue to a formal agreement.

From that day in the early '80s forward, I continued to insist on either an MOU or Agreement in Principle be drafted before proceeding to a formal agreement. That is, except for one time in 2005. The deal was so large and it was the first for our new startup, so I gave in to the statement, "this is the agreement we have used many times and any OEM agreements must be signed on this paper". This lapse on my decades of insistence on the business points be ironed out first, cost us four months of legal back and forth. This was required to get a balanced agreement. No one would have signed what originally came from their legal – totally one sided. When you are a new startup and this is your first big deal, those four months are critical to cash flow. After the agreement was signed, another four months were spent demonstrating we had the manufacturing capability and quality control to execute on the agreement.

Non Disclosures – Confidential Agreements

Non Disclosure agreements are required when two companies have reason to discuss or negotiate at the detail level. The NDA is worded to protect the intellectual property, designs, business intent or anything that one or both parties wish to remain confidential.

In the hi-tech industry these are very common. Sometimes these are simple agreements of only a few pages and sometimes if there are defined periods that the information must not be revealed or there are consequences for disclosure included, they may be longer.

Looking back on the NDAs I have kept, there are some very standard ones. These are usually signed when the company giving information wants the receiving company to keep any information delivered not be disclosed to any other party outside their company. This is a very common case when more detail is requested on new products or technologies – an example of a one-way relay of confidential information.

Many times each party may reveal confidential information to the other. So, there are Mutual Non Discloser Agreements – MNDA's.

How many agreements were personally worked on in the five decades of my business career? No exact number, but there were many agreements from each of these companies: NAS, Intel, ECD, Motorola, Decision Data, DataQuest, CoreData, Sterling Software, Computer Associates, personal consulting agreements, and HierStar. Including all of the MOUs, NDAs as well as definitive formal agreements, the number is in the hundreds.

Lesson 22: Remember everyone who is interested may not be worth your time.
Know when not to contract. If you have a hot new technology or product, "interested parties" seem to come out of the woodwork. This requires a sorting of genuinely good potential clients from the lookers,

curious students, unfunded startups, and potential corporate spies.

Time is precious. It shouldn't be wasted and that is what some of the "lookers" may be doing. So, it's necessary to qualify interested parties to determine – what is in this interaction for my company? It takes very little time to send a standard NDA to an interested party, and once it is signed and returned, to send out the standard information packet. However, even this routine function can take too much time and money. So, again – qualify the request. Ask what they plan to do with the information (once they have signed and returned an NDA). Do they have competing products, are they inquiring for information only? Information only requests – send to your web site.

A more insidious waste of time is the "potential partner" whose business is related to your focus and goals only tangentially. Particularly, startups are susceptible to being taken off target by what seems to be an extra revenue source. Personally, I have experienced this with the cofounder in my last startup – he was too easily swayed to move off our focus when he thought he saw "easy money". He seemed to have the WW II bomber waist gunner mentality. They would shoot at anything that might fly by. Their motto was – we shoot 'em down, you sort 'em out on the ground".

This lack of focus on your strategic goals and objectives can be very dangerous and costly. Be careful not to chase what is not worth catching.

10 NEGOTIATING A SALE OR MERGER
LESSON 23:

It's an exciting time, when a young company is looking for a partner to buy or merge with them. Finally, some reward for the demanding work schedule of a startup. But how do you go about finding a buyer for your company?

If you have a technology startup company, then your product technology must have found a niche that the big guys (larger companies) have not filled yet. If you are a more mature company, you may have an established product with a larger installed base of users. I have seen both of these cases and found buyers.

Best candidates – make your list
The first step should be to make a list of the best candidates to be your merger partner or buyer. Best candidates could be companies that are maybe your

customers, or companies in the same market space, or even competitors. Make a list of the top 10 – 12 candidates.

Strategic fit candidates

What is the strategic fit with each company's product line? In one example, the potential buyers had storage management software including risk management software – essentially managed backup. Their market was the data centers and distributed systems requiring central storage management. They were missing all of the data residing on the remote workers laptops, which were effectively unmanaged. And the amount of data that represented was significant and important; it would increase the amount of data center information they could manage.

Our young company had some interesting backup software for remote laptops. The software automatically backed up only the changed bytes of data from the time it was last backed up to now. It did not require the laptop user, or road warrior, as they were called, to remember to run a backup; it was performed automatically and transmitted to the company's central site whenever the user contacted the home system.

Companies in the data management software space were all a potential strategic fit to use the new company's leading edge remote backup software. This category of companies made up half of the list of 10 -12 potential candidates. All of the candidates of course were large companies and in competition with each other.

Make the big guys fear what you may do
To me, this was an interesting thought. What might the larger storage management companies fear? Well, at least some of them might fear losing out on managing the large amount of the data that existed on their customers remote laptop users systems. Additionally, they might fear being short on the check list of what features customers might specify on their next bid for storage management software. They might fear that if they didn't have the remote capability, then their competition might. Would that make it harder to compete?

Installed customer base as a lever
In one case in my experience, the company to be sold had several well entrenched products installed in a large number of customers – some very prestigious ones too. The lever in negotiations with potential buyers was the installed customer base. A buyer imagines selling more products into that base where a customer/vendor relationship has already been established. The customer knows the product(s) and a working relationship exists

with the vendor of those products. If enough of the selling company's employees are kept on, then there might be a seamless transition to the new vendor.

Sometimes your best customer may be a good candidate

In some cases, a large company fueled the development of our startup's product. As a customer and a user, they would be in a good position to dictate the direction of the product features. If the startup's product was strategic enough for this sponsor, might they want to keep it from their competitors? If so, they also are on the list of potential buyers. Many startups have been funded this way, and some may even have been merged into the sponsoring company.

A competitor may be a good candidate

Maybe there is a well funded competitor that would like to eliminate your company as its competition. Some of these may find their way on your candidate list too. Interfacing with competitors during a purchase or buy out can be very tricky. In the process of presenting "why buy me" they will learn too much confidential and sensitive information like your patent position, key employees, customers and best prospects, partners your have and more. A direct interface to these candidates is not recommended from my experience.

Use a third party

In these case,I have successfully used a third party company to interface between the seller and potential buyer as in the case above. Of course, when your competitors are on your candidate list I feel this is a must. A third party (there are many companies specializing in this work), can keep the selling companies name out of discussions until appropriate interest has been generated and the proper NDA's are executed. In addition, as negotiations proceed, their role becomes the "net man' the negotiations. This helps keep emotions out of the process as each party may send the "net man" back and forth to represent their case.

Caution – watch out for loose cannons

Negotiations are going well. Additional information has been requested and supplied. A rapport has developed. Discussions regarding employees had commenced. It seems like it is going to be a GO.

From personal experience – there was one little glitch. The negotiations were down to the last days. Then, a person recently fired from the company being acquired, turned hostile. This person loved guns and used to show everyone in the office his gun catalogues. He used to recount his experiences on the firing ranges.

Within a day or two after his firing he began calling some key people at the office with threats of violence both in the office and at or around their homes. These telephone and email threats were specific and had to be taken seriously. The buying company had to be told and they were. But, it was also explained what measures were being taken to protect people and property. One of the measures was to have an armed guard at our office entrance each day to discourage any violence and to give a reasonable amount of relief to employees. It worked. The purchase was completed without further incident. Whew!

11 STARTUPS & FUNDING SOURCES
LESSON 24:

You have the next great product idea and it might become a success, if you could only get the company started. Test your Product and Market Attractiveness with the matrix in Exhibit 11.1

Start-up companies were some of the most exciting times during those 50 years. They required a lot of long hours and were risky to say the least. Some questions that are always asked are:

Will we get funded?
How and by whom?
Will the funding source want too much ownership of the company?
Etc.

If you have a good product or service idea, and have a business plan that makes a good case for why your company will be successful, against existing or presumed competition, where do you turn for money? It should be said here that any source of outside funding will want to see that your team has some "skin in the game". Having some of the team's assets invested demonstrates that you are willing to risk money on this venture. Now, would the outside funding like to join in? Personally, I have experienced several ways of funding a startup company.

Internal company funding
My first startup venture, was an internal startup at Intel. Intel treated the business plan just like a Venture Capital company might. If you are able to present a good enough case to get some seed money, additional funding will depend on attaining milestones of performance or achievements before follow-on cash is available. The first seed funding set up the internal startup as a "separate company" inside Intel, with the startup's staffing, and with its board made up of several Intel executives. The incentive for the startup team was an ownership of the profits of the venture once (and if) it became profitable.

To get operations funding, the startup had to develop prototypes with the seed money and obtain orders from key (named) interested prospects. Those orders, if secured, would bring more significant investment to go into additional engineering, product manufacturing and marketing.

The startup product did get orders from major prospects and the operation became a separate company inside Intel.

As a source of funding this is a great one! They already know you and your ability and are willing to make a bet on your new "world beating idea". However, this source of funding is probably the least common.

Your customer(s) as a funding source
Maybe, you already have a customer who has paid for you to develop a generalized product or service. This payment would come as orders for completed product stages and billed to the customer as completed. What is in it for this customer(s)? Well, he gets the opportunity to direct the features and user interfaces he requires for his business and doesn't have to try to fit into some standard product or software package. Also, the pioneering customer will likely get special pricing and/or other terms that benefit him in addition to the prospect of being first in the market with the new capability.

Assuming the ownership is yours and not the paying customer (this will be determined by the agreement between the parties), then the resulting product is yours to market to the broader market. One software startup I was in used this approach. Within a little over two years, the startup became profitable and within about three years was purchased by a larger company who saw it as a strategic fit with their products.

Self funding

The last hi tech startup I founded received its startup funding from the founders and other initial employees (who were all on the board as well). Very quickly though, we secured orders from a large company in the security software business, and we were on our way.

Venture Capital funding - VCs

VCs are similar to banks – if you don't really need the money, then they want to give you some.

The batting average for success of a VC funded company is 1 in 10 (a resounding .100 batting average). That must be the reason that this source is first of all, hard to convince to fund your plan and if they do, they want too much ownership. They see so many company presentations asking for funding that it is hard to get their attention – we've seen that idea already. But, they make a lot of mistakes too. They pass on many plans that will eventually become successful and fund many who turn out to be disasters. The many dot com companies were an example of a major series of disasters. (There were so many VC funded dot.com companies out of business in Silicon Valley, that furniture from the empty offices had to be almost given away to clear space).

My score card is not very good on VC funding. The first business plan I shopped was in October of 1987 – just before "black Monday" market crash. The plan was for a multiprocessor server, and it did get funding eventually.

Another great idea that didn't get funding from VCs, was a plan to develop a technology vendor service that would illustrate what the "best practice" information technology end users were doing to maximize their information system investment. In other words, sell the technology companies information about how the best users were using their competitor's products. This of course, was to learn what they had to do to compete. Later, almost the exact same idea was funded with a name eerily familiar to the one I had presented.

Here's what the VCs are looking for

1. A strong management team with a proven track record of success
2. A plan that clearly shows your "idea" will fill a market space of significant size, and generate a growing revenue stream
3. Some proof that prospects will sign up – could be that you already have an initial customer or two using your product idea
4. Prototypes that can demonstrate your "ground breaking" product

5. Defendable rationale that major competitive companies (or just large companies in your general market) won't prevent your success
6. VCs like to see factors of 10 – that is 10x performance, 1/10 the price etc.
7. A potential fit with other companies in their funded portfolio

Remember the end game of the VC is to profit when your company goes public or gets a good purchase offer.

Angel Funding

Angels are individuals or small groups that are looking for good investments that will not require significant cash requirements. Their plan is to get a new company to the point where VCs or prospective buyer may find them attractive. Therefore, the Angel gets a good investment return. Many Angel investors have run companies, have management experience in startups and have good connections to VCs.

Spin outs

Another type of startup, or at least new venture type company, involves a division of a larger company that is seeking funding for expanding operations. This expansion funding would be used for completing engineering tasks and setting up manufacturing and marketing/sales.

Generally, these spin outs will offer their own securities, like an IPO, to operate separately from their parent. I was involved in securing spin out funding for an innovative LCD technology. The chief scientist and I made the Wall Street tour of four cities. We presented to investment bankers in New York, Boston, Philadelphia, and Minneapolis. Within about four months that tour yielded $23M and allowed the division to successfully set up a new separate company.

The last startup I was involved as a cofounder, was a network security company. It was quite different because it involved incorporating in the U.S., Hong Kong, and China (PRC). There is a little more to say about that in the Chapter 13 - Extra Lessons.

12 EMPLOYEE MOTIVATION
LESSON 25:

Motivation comes in short bursts –act while it's hot!

Good News Meetings

Motivating of your employees seems more like an art rather than a science. People are not the same and they may not be motivated the same way as others. When there has been some significant change in the company or group, many in the group are wondering –"what's my future here, "are we still a viable operation", "should I dust off my resume?". In my experience, I have had to sell operations and relocate people, take over from another GM, recoup morale when popular employees were released because drug issues, and attempt to rekindle morale in an operation that has always lost money.

First of all, being positive and bringing out positive news

seemed to be important in enhancing employee morale and motivation.

With that thought, the monthly "Good News", meetings were born. People genuinely like to hear positive news – good news. They like to hear people recognized for specific work related successes – and they hope to be recognized sometime too. As the GM of an operation of over 200 people, mostly engineering and marketing types, I attempted to put together what was going right and what needed to be improved in the form of a Good News presentation.

Here were the aspects of the meeting format.

1. Report on the successes of the operations performance against goal – Good News
2. Where there was a miss against goals, concentrate on presenting it as a "where we can improve". Where can you help to improve performance on that goal/objective?
3. Have each manager – hardware engineering, quality control, software engineering, manufacturing engineering, marketing, etc., report on one or two instances he observed of a specific employees' "above and beyond" performance. Then specifically, illustrate how that performance was contributing to goal attainment

for the operation. This was done by each manager in front of the assembled group.
4. Finally, in the meeting, set the direction toward achieving the "need to improve goals".
5. The day following the Good News recognition of an employees' performance, the GM would seek out the contributor at his work and personally thank him/her. It seemed to be important to do this in the work setting and around their fellow employees.

Importance of quarterly Objectives and Key Results

The importance of establishing each employees objectives and key results for each quarter, form a culture of personal accountability, as has been mentioned earlier. But it is important to employee motivation and morale too. Employees ask themselves questions like: "What do I have to do to succeed in this job?" What do I have to do to get a promotion or higher pay?"

Remember these key results or action steps were reviewed each month in an employee one-on-one with his manager and graded each quarter. At that time, the employee knows where he stands regarding the questions above, and what is required to achieve his personal goals. At the same meeting, objectives and key results are set for the next quarter. The employee and the manager set these points together, with buy in from the employee. Some employees will even set their goals very high for the next quarter. That's a good thing, but it is up to the manager to keep them realistic.

This process points out clearly what success looks like and what it takes to move up in the group. This process fits nicely with the culture of moving decision making to the lowest level possible. Together, they give enhanced job satisfaction and a feeling of accomplishment – personal motivation.

Motivation in Bad Business Times

Periods when a company is in difficult times is when employee motivation and morale is really tested. The hard times might be because of a competitor's actions, or failed product launch or actions by the government or many other things. The question becomes will employees still pull together? Will they be willing to do more or something "special" if required?

I have observed this several times. The challenge was identified, the sacrifice was outlined and the employees were asked to meet the challenge. In the early Intel days, there were several large Japanese semiconductor companies that challenged Intel's ability to succeed in its markets. The "enemy" had more money, more engineers and more fabrication plants. But there was opportunity to surprise them with Intel's agility in achieving high yields quicker on new products that would be very competitive. But to do that would take a sacrifice from all employees, even those not in the chip side of the business.

From what I observed, Intel did these things right:

1. **Identified the enemy (specific Japanese semiconductor companies)**
2. **outlined specifically, the type, size and scope of the required employee sacrifice.**
3. **Kept their word on what they required of employees and how long it would last.**

In order to generate faster performance to attain high yield on the key chip components, Intel instituted **the 125% Solution**. This required that all employees work 25% more hours per week for a specified period of time at the same pay.

On another occasion, operating cash was the issue. A program called **the 90% Solution** was launched. It required all employees take a 10% pay cut for a specified period of time. Gee…why doesn't our government think like that?

Both programs were successful at providing Intel what was needed. And at the end of each program there was a "celebration" with mementos for all.

Morale and enthusiasm was maintained by targeting a specific "enemy", and being clear on when the sacrifices would end.

You can't motivate those who will not be motivated
Remember some of those employees that you couldn't seem to motivate? Well, maybe it is them not you. I remember hiring in L.A. and experiencing the "L. A. complex". Los Angeles, like no other place I have experienced, seems to have a lot of the unmotivated. In one capacity, I would go out for a day with my salesmen and make calls they had scheduled. A motivated salesman knows his territory, has objectives and a plan for the day – especially when the boss in coming. Not always true in L.A. One salesman really demonstrated that – couldn't find the customer we were to call on, had no objectives for his calls and no plan.

Once when interviewing for new salesmen in L.A., a young women interviewed. It wasn't a good interview, and I wasn't tempted to hire her. However, she did send me a follow-up thank you card. The card was of her in a bikini and said thanks for the interview. Was her motivation to get hired? Would she have been a good performer if hired? Probably not is the answer to these questions – but just another example of trying to find motivated employees in L.A.

13 *EXTRA LESSON*
DOING BUSINESS IN CHINA

The last eight years of my business life was dedicated to co-founding, funding and building a business that was incorporated in the U.S., Hong Kong and China. In this extra lesson chapter, several of the important things to consider before launching into such a far flung venture are outlined here.

What is so different about doing business in China? Here are some things to consider:

1. If you establish your engineering and manufacturing in China, you are a foreign company – even if some of your ownership in Chinese.

2. The cost of incorporation is not cheap like in the U.S. In this venture we established three

companies in China and paid 4 million Yuan, or RMB to establish each.

3. The government can turn on a dime and change things that will affect you drastically. A couple of examples – the holding period before you can sell your real estate, and the labor laws, which will significantly affect your bottom line.

4. How will you get your money out of China? It is difficult to get Yuan out of China, so that was one of the reasons to establish a HK headquarters office for the Hong Kong company. Orders from our customers were placed on HK and the China companies were contracted to fulfill the order.

5. Everything you have heard about the difficulty in protecting your Intellectual Property is true. We developed and had issued 17 patents. When a couple of employees left, so did some patents on plastic molding. Copying your products by a company down the street is common and an acceptable business practice. Not too many lawyers in China, and seldom is legal action taken.

6. The lines of communication are long between

countries. The opportunities for misunderstanding are huge – and the language difference can't be over stated.

7. There is almost a cultural issue with establishing effective quality assurance programs for your engineering and manufacturing.

8. Most of our security products were sold outside of China – U.S., Europe, Japan, Israel etc. Attempts to sell in China were met with the "bribe me" if you want the order syndrome. This was very open and everyone knew it was expected.

9. Then of course the government, (including the local ones), seem to always have their hands out for fees whenever you want to do anything. Plant inspections are a veil for a "hand outs to government".

10. A final word must be said in the defense of the hardworking Chinese people. Never, Never have I worked with an engineering, and management crew who worked so hard and so long for our company. That type of hard work has paid off handsomely for many factory owners.

I enjoyed the China venture tremendously though. It was an example of growing an engineering, manufacturing, and software company, to profit in just over a year. The culture, the architecture of China and the food (some, not all) were wonderful adventures.

Many have reported on the vast new manufacturing complexes the government built to encourage businesses where there were lots of villagers that needed work. Also, I saw cases of over building where entire complexes of buildings were vacant.

I watched buildings being built, and 40-story buildings having their windows washed. But the amazing thing about these scenes to me was this – the scaffolding on high rise buildings under construction was bamboo, and the window washers were hanging on one long knotted rope (no safety harness or rope) as they washed their way down from the top floors. Easy to find replacements if …….

A meeting with the immigration police
One of our offices was in Beijing. The summer before the Olympics I traveled to Beijing. I had stayed in hotels before, but because we had recently purchased condos behind our office building, I stayed there.

The next morning, I was in the office about an hour when I was told there were six immigration police at the front that wished to see me. Imagine, six police coming to see just one of me.

The story was that I had forgotten to file a paper with the police on where I would be staying in Beijing after arrival. Normally, the hotel files that paper if you stay in a hotel. To me the whole thing seemed funny – six came to pick me up. So, I asked if one of our folks at the front desk would take a picture of me with the six police – all smiling. They assured me that would not be a good idea and so I went along with the program and filed the paper with the local police station.

There were many interesting occurrences during my trips and visits in China, but maybe later I will revisit some of those.

14 CONCLUSION PERSPECTIVE & EXHIBITS:

This is the first book I have ever written and it provided me with the opportunity to look back, and review my life. Did I sacrifice too much in pursuing my goals? After all there were 16 moves, and I was on the other end in the new job for sometimes as long as a year before the family could move. My son was in three high schools in four years – that must have been pretty rough.

Once when my daughter was only three, she noticed that Mommy was furiously cleaning the house and straightening up – back to the model home look. She said, "Mom are we having an open house (meaning are we selling and moving again) or is grandma coming?"

I was pursuing my dream, but was the cost to my family too great? My kids tell me that one of the advantages to moving so much was that they got good at introducing themselves.

In the process of writing this book, I was amazed to recall how much of technology industry history I observed – up close and personal.

My first machines to work with were 80 column card unit record machines. Then there were all of the incompatible programmable systems, then the mainframe systems families and finally the personal computers and handheld devices.

The products of the last security startup included a complete computer – processing, memory, storage, display, input and communications in a form factor that was within the normal bank credit card. This product was on its way to becoming one of the solutions to Internet fraud. Its purpose was to authenticate the user – establish his true identity with the bank's or his enterprise's server. But the bank problems of 2008 dealt a serious blow to our largest potential customers.

Recently, there was a piece on the news with a security expert relating the importance of such capabilities – they are now common in Europe and Asia. Maybe we were a little too early, before that market took off, but I believe you will have a device like this in your hands for your banking and online purchasing someday soon.

Some of the illustrations in this chapter may help clarify the text, and give the credibility to my journey. It happened as I reported. I lived it, move by move, company by company, technology by technology and crisis by crisis, and celebration after celebration.

25 Lessons Learned from 50 Years in Hi Tech

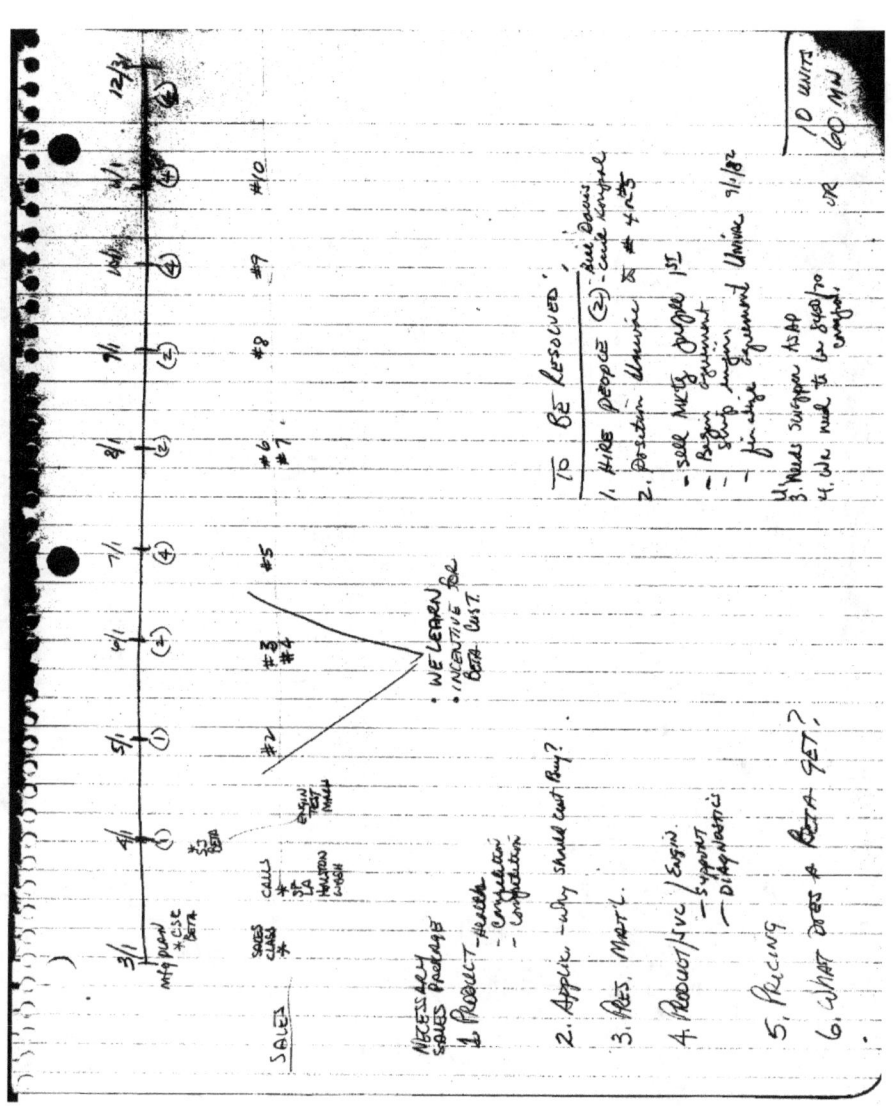

EHIBIT 3.1

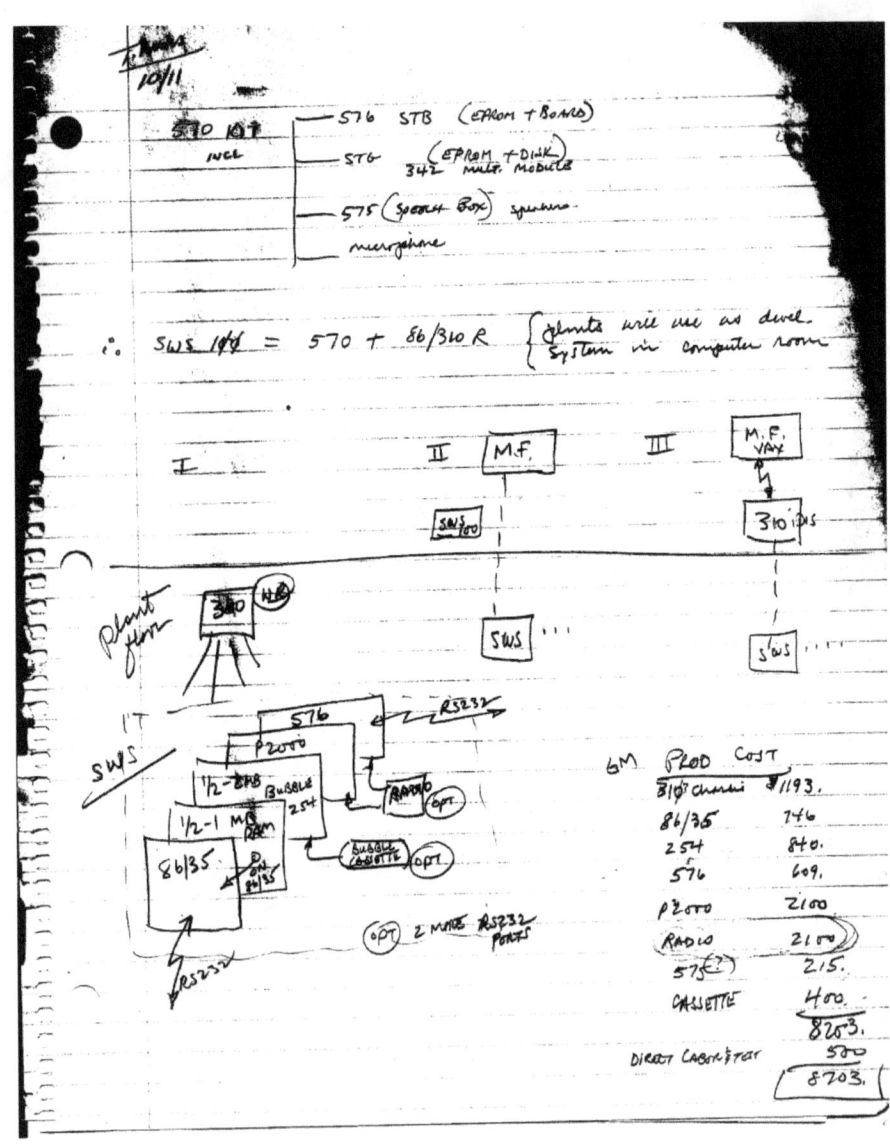

EXHIBIT 3.2

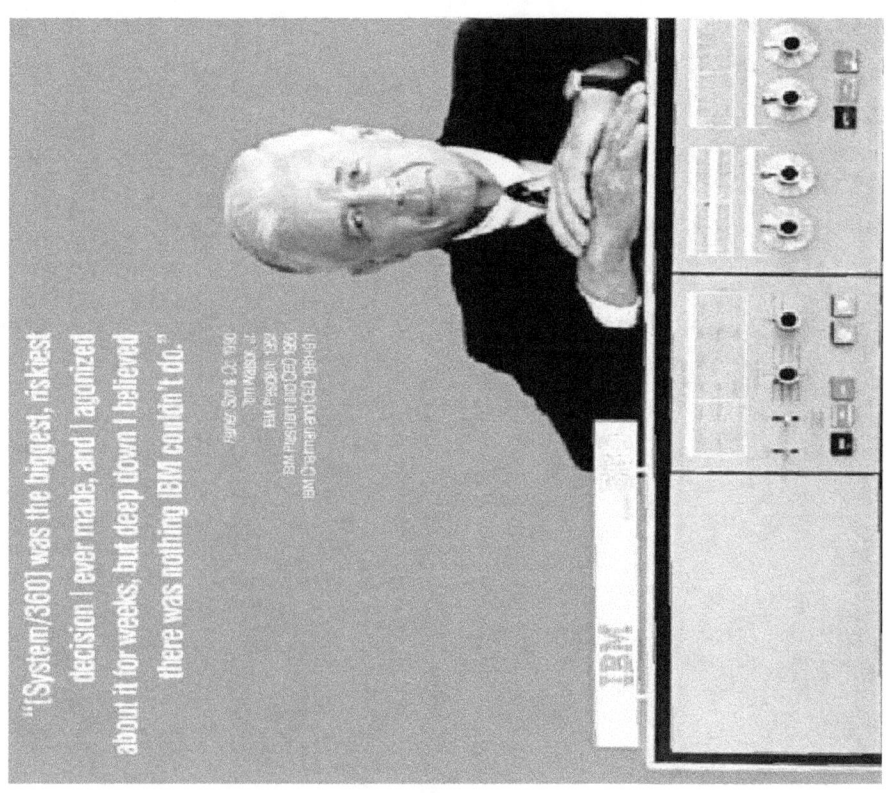

T.J. WATSON JR.
REGARDING THE S/360 DECISION

Bob W   C/WL
             CONF

Just a note to thank you for being a real trooper and handling some of the trickiest tasks a GM ever faces.

I really appreciate your efforts and am rooting for/with you!

Regards,

A.S. Grove

ANDY GROVE ATTA' BOY NOTE
EXHIBIT 7.1

THE SALES FUNNEL

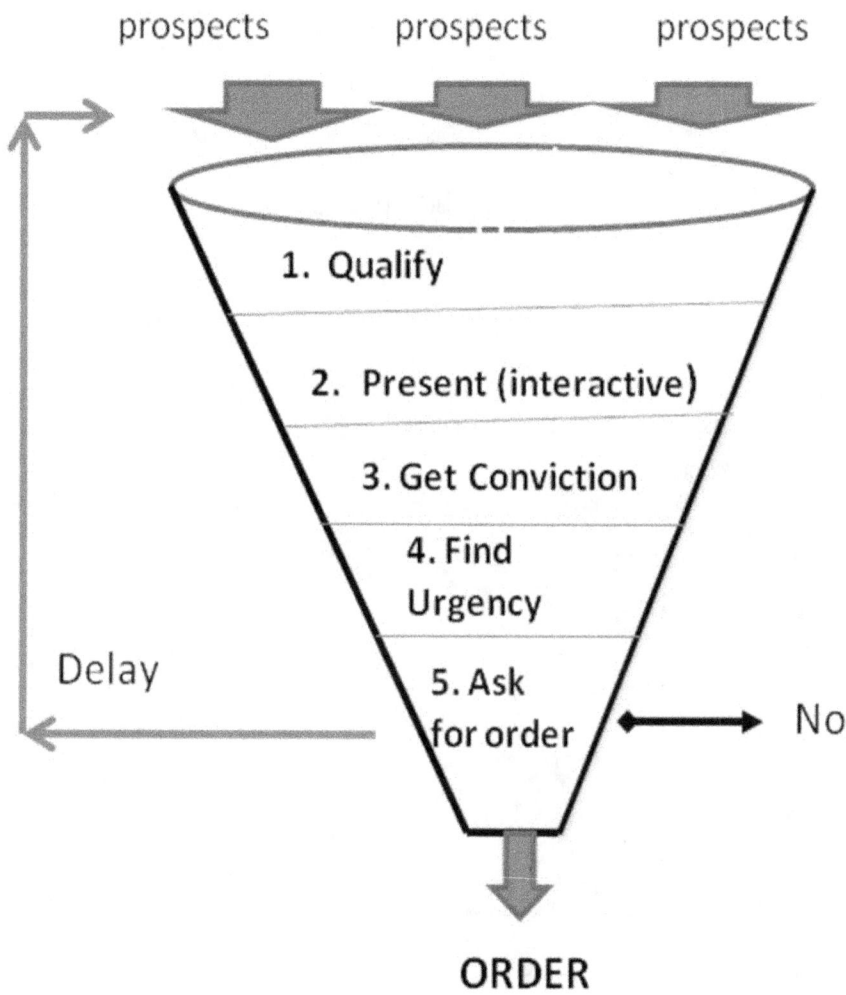

EXHIBIT 5.1

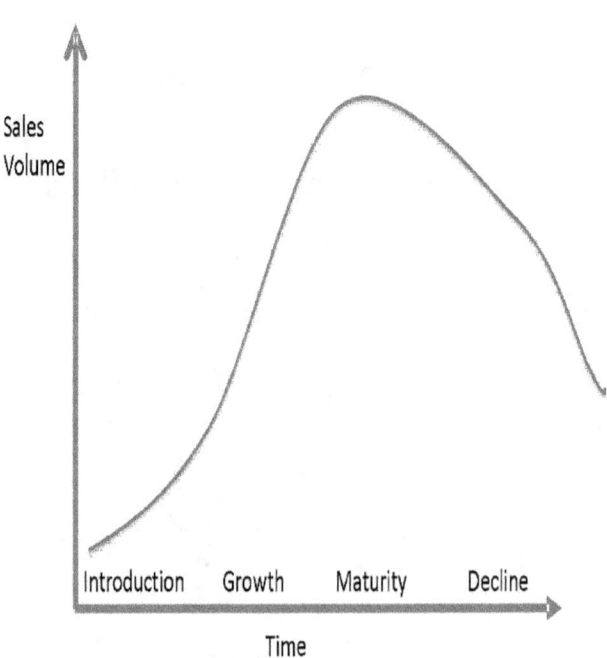

EXHIBIT 11.1

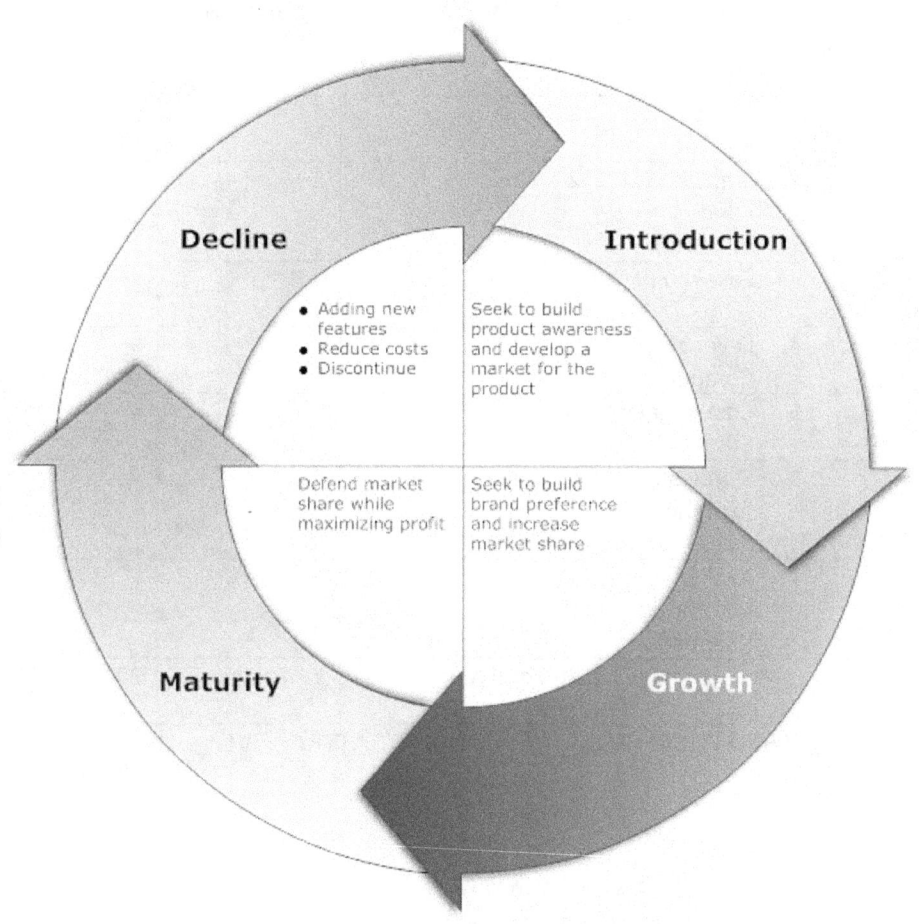

EXHIBIT 11.2

PRODUCT/MARKET	ATTRACTIVENESS	MATRIX	
Attractiveness Features	*Product Idea 1*	*Competitor A*	*Competitor B*
1. Size of Market	5	4	3
2. Startup Funds Required	2	2	2
3. Ease of Entry	3	3	2
4. Level of Compet.	5	4	5
5. Cost of Sales Efforts	4	3	4
6. Opportunity for Quick Sales	4	2	2
7. Avail of Distribution Channels	3	4	2
	26 Total	22 Total	20 Total

1 = LEAST ATTRACTIVE   5 = MOST ATTRACTIVE

EXHIBIT 11.3

MEMORANDUM OF UNDERSTANDING

This Memorandum of Understanding ("*MOU*") is entered into as of April __, 20xx (the "*Effective Date*") by and between,   and   , the *Parties*.

SCOPE

Intent Representatives of company A and company B have been agreed in principle to establish a strategic relationship in which company A will represent company B China software development expertise in North America. The purpose of this MOU is to confirm the current status of discussions and to provide a framework within which company A and company B will work together. The Parties intend to proceed to negotiate one or more definitive agreements (collectively, "*Definitive Agreements*") to be approved by both Parties.

Company A

A is organized and staffed to find and contract new clients for outsourcing to one or more labs in China. Representation of Chinese labs will principally be in the areas of storage and security technologies with the intent of developing deeper domain expertise in the technology focus areas. In addition, A will manage the on-going relationship with clients, with the intent to preserve and grow revenue for its strategic partner labs. A currently has staff in Maryland and California.

Company B

B is organized to provide technical software related skills to clients in North America from its offices and labs in China. B currently has approximately four clients in North America and an administrative office in Palo Alto, CA.

Objectives:

A and B have agreed on the following objectives of the relationship.
- A. A for consideration, will represent B as their exclusive sales and marketing agent in North America to current and future clients.

- B. A will endeavor to use the experience and skill of its staff to focus on new and/or add-on project work for B in the focus areas agreed upon by the parties (see attachment 1) in order to increase the domain expertise of the B staff.

- C. A will use the experience and skill of its staff to increase the revenue for B

- D. A will use the experience and skill of its staff to increase the number of B Clients in North America.

- E. In consideration for this representation by A, B will establish A as the sole sales, marketing and customer contact to its current and new customers.

TERMS OF THIS MOU:

Infrastructure   The parties agree to work together to provide collaboration software in order to allow   proposing and on-going customer project status with agreed upon status Gant or Pert charts as presently   used by B. The Parties further agree to set regular management meetings and to cooperate on   web content on the A web site to appropriately represent the B professional services   laboratories.

Company A responsibilities
A as the client consultant, will be responsible to represent the range of services provided by B for software development, QA & testing, prototyping and other such services that are consistent with the skills and experience of B. A will work with the client to define a Statement of Work and work with B in order to produce a client proposal for services and then propose and invoice clients.

A will interface with current customers to solidify the relationship and enhance the opportunities for project extension and the addition of new projects.

A will monitor on-going client projects.

A will be responsible for billing and collection from clients for service work performed by B, and remit 60% of new client revenue to B, as collected from clients.

Company B Responsibilities
B will provide a skills document that adequately describes the skilled services they can provide.

B will provide development project management, project manpower loading and costing and on-going project status. They will cooperate with A to agree on when project managers will visit clients.

B will negotiate with A a reasonable fee for the management of some or all current clients that are producing revenue.

Marketing and Sales approach B agrees that A will be responsible for sales, marketing, primary customer management and that all new agreements with be written by A on their agreement paper and will clearly identify B laboratories as the services provider.

Company A   **Company B**

By:_____   By:_____

Title:_____   Title:_____

EXHIBIT 9.1

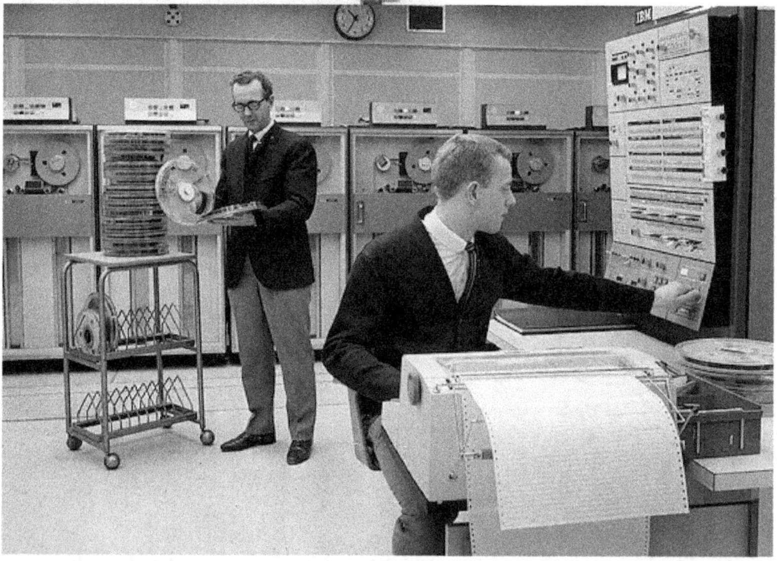

25 Lessons Learned from 50 Years in Hi Tech

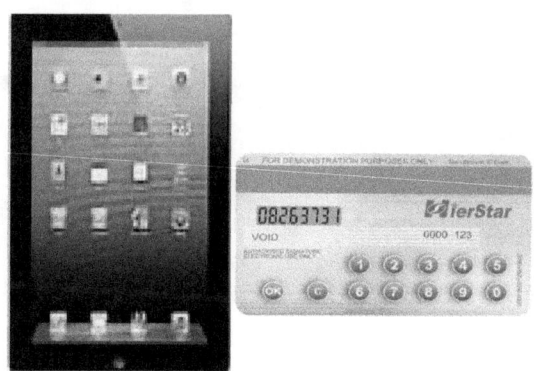

EVOLUTION OF COMPUTING OVER 50 YEARS

MINIMAL IBM 1401 SYSTEM – EARLY 1960'S

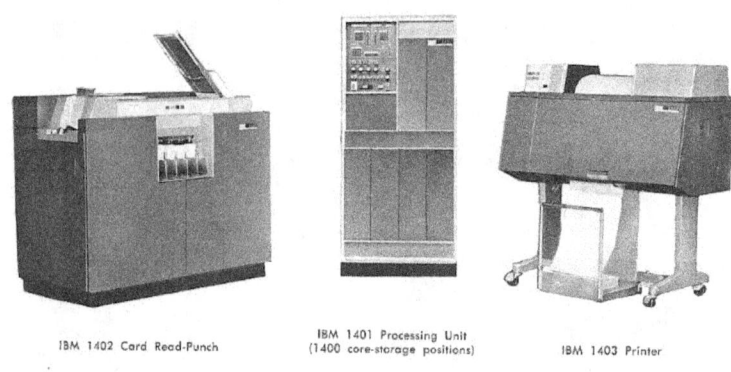

IBM 1402 Card Read-Punch   IBM 1401 Processing Unit (1400 core-storage positions)   IBM 1403 Printer

The 1401 System was the first system I installed as an IBM S.E.

EVOLUTION OF COMPUTING OVER 50 YEARS

Comparison

IBM 1401 Computer System Modern PC

Attribute	IBM 1401	Modern PC
Computer	Yes	Yes
Memory	Core	Dynamic RAM
Memory Size	16K	I Gig
Speed	1x	10,000x
In use	2?	Billions
Size	One large bedroom	In briefcase
Power	3 Households	60 Watt bulb
Cost (new)	1 airplane	1 bicycle

EVOLUTION OF COMPUTING OVER 50 YEARS

EVOLUTION OF COMPUTING OVER 50 YEARS

EVOLUTION OF COMPUTING OVER 50 YEARS

IT SEEMED LIKE A LONG JOURNEY
– BUT WORTH IT.

ABOUT THE AUTHOR

The author now lives once again in northern California, where he arrived after sixteen business moves across the country. Other than the time spent on this first book, he enjoys golf, traveling, and volunteering to help kindergarten students in reading and math.

25 Lessons Learned from 50 Years in Hi Tech

www.ingramcontent.com/pod-product-compliance
Lightning Source LLC
Chambersburg PA
CBHW051653170526
45167CB00001B/454